C000229051

0 862 999 340 428 69

NOTTINGHAMSHIRE COUNTY COUNCIL
COMMUNITY SERVICES - LIBRARIES

90p

WITHDRAWN FOR RE-SALE

SOLD

GRAIN AND CHAFF UNDER THE HILL

To Elsie, my wife –
but for her encouragement and help,
this book would never have been
written.

GRAIN AND CHAFF UNDER THE HILL

FRED ◆ ARCHER

Nottinghamshire County Council
942.449
15028428
Leisure Services/Libraries

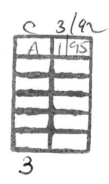

C 3/92
A 1 95

3

ALAN SUTTON

First published in the United Kingdom in 1991
Alan Sutton Publishing Limited · Phoenix Mill · Far Thrupp
Stroud · Gloucestershire

First published in the United States of America in 1992
Alan Sutton Publishing Inc · Wolfeboro Falls · NH 03896–0848

Copyright © Fred Archer, 1991

All rights reserved. No part of this publication may be
reproduced, stored in a retrieval system, or transmitted, in any
form or by any means, electronic, mechanical, photocopying,
recording or otherwise, without the prior permission of the
publishers and copyright holders.

British Library Cataloguing in Publication Data

Archer, Fred, *1915–*
Grain and chaff under the hill
I. Title
942.449

ISBN 0-86299-934-0

Library of Congress Cataloging in Publication Data applied for

Typeset in Bembo 11/14.
Typesetting and origination by
Alan Sutton Publishing Ltd.
Printed in Great Britain by
The Bath Press, Bath, Avon.

Contents

———

CONTENTS

Introduction

In *Under Milk Wood* Dylan Thomas writes 'If you have lived in one village you have lived in the lot.' There are similar characters in all villages. He writes of Waldro and his Guinness with an egg in it and the Maternity Order; Evans the Post steaming the letters open and little Polly Garter always having babies. She says, 'Isn't life terrible, thank God.' We who experienced village life in the 1920s have met folk of a similar ilk to Dylan's characters.

The question has often been asked of me, 'Is life better or worse than it was in the 1920s?' My answer is that it is neither better nor worse, but so different it's like living on another planet.

Men worked harder on the land than they do today yet life went on at a slower pace. Horses were the main source of power in the fields – draught animals. The farmworker worked alongside, lifting great weights, bending, pulling, always using muscle power, walking miles to plough an acre. Today I wonder whether it was sensible for men to carry $2\frac{1}{4}$ cwt sacks of wheat up stone steps into a granary, yet men who couldn't were reckoned to be second class.

The dress of the farm worker then was so different from today. Ploughmen wore breeches and leggings in winter and hob-nailed boots. Walking miles as they did behind the plough on wet clay land or stony hill, the dress was sensible. Ploughmen today wear boiler suits over their clothes, protection from oil, dust and fuel, tidy without any clothing being loose to catch in moving parts on machinery.

The older men in the 1920s wore corduroy trousers with yorks, or straps, below the knee to give a little fullness when they were working. Summer clothes were not that different but on the hayfield or at harvest straw hats were common, a good protection from the sun and also from the hayseeds when they were roping the wagon-loads of hay. I only ever saw one farm worker working hatless in the fields. Everyone wore either a cap or a hat. Battered greasy trilbies seemed to predominate. It was essential to have a good pair of boots, watertight, but many went home with wet feet in that time before Wellington boots were available.

There was a terrific community spirit on the land all those years ago. Very few of the workers belonged to a trade union but they did stand together doing their best to bargain with their employers. They still talked of Joseph Arch, the Warwickshire hedge layer, but they didn't really trust the authority of union leaders.

Wages in the 1920s were poor – at thirty shillings for a week of fifty-two hours and ninepence an hour for overtime – men were worse off than their fathers were before the First World War. They had earned sixteen shillings a week, but food was cheaper and rents negligible.

George Ewart Evans writes of the oral tradition, and he is so right. It would be hard to exaggerate the value of words handed down from father to son, which became the Bible of life on the land. No man planted his potatoes on the allotments until Good Friday, no farmer turned his cattle out of the yard to the fields until May Day.

Back in the 1920s it was quite easy to discern which village a person came from by their speech and examples of dialect were easy to come by. In the market expressions like 'Ast planted thee snips yet?' (Have you planted your parsnips yet?), 'Smartish frost isterdey marning. Dost reckon it killed the blow?' (A sharp frost yesterday morning. Do you think it has killed the plum blossom?) were common. Some expressions used by the workers on the land originated with Shakespeare and the King James Bible. The word 'filler' used to describe the horse next to the plough in the team or the shaft horse in a cart or wagon, was used in an earlier form by Shakespeare in *The Merchant of Venice* when Old Gobbo said, 'Thou hast got more hair on thy chin than Dobbin my thill-horse has on his tail.' 'Anant' used so often in the Vale of Evesham, was used by the monks in Pershore Abbey. The words of the Carter to me as a plough boy still ring in my ears. 'Get up anant them 'osses.'

Neddy Slap, a character early in this century, came to work one morning and said to my uncle, 'The missus had a babby last night, just like a rot. Thee guess what it was.'

'A bwoy,' my uncle replied.

'No. Thee guess agyun.'

'A girl,' the reply came.

'Somebody must have telled tha,' Neddy replied.

One benefit I enjoyed as a boy, being the son of a farmer, was what I call listening to the 'Wisdom of the Ancients'. On wet days in the granary, the shepherd and the cowman would be kibbling those flat board-like slabs of cattle cake, linseed and cotton cake for the sheep and the cattle. In the corner of the granary old Jack Fox would be making pegs for rabbit snares from a piece of straight grained ash he had put by months, maybe years, before. Jack gleaned his wood from the hedgerows, and with sharp tools made shafts for hay forks, axes, etc. Jack was called a rough carpenter but he wasn't rough in my book. On those wet days I took a turn on the cake kibbler but was soon out of puff. It gave the shepherd time to charge his clay pipe with Shag tobacco. The conversation between these men was usually of 'The Old Times', and was very critical of today.

'Education is no good on to chaps who be gwain to work on the land,' the shepherd commented. 'Now they goes to the Grammar School and thinks they knows everything. I left the village school at eleven year old and thee send one of them at sixteen singling mangolds along of me, that's a different kettle of fish!'

The cowman then turned to the subject of beer. 'It unt like it used to be, you knows that Jack.'

Jack put his hatchet down replying, 'Beer! They don't know what beer is today. Chaps today be weak in the yud. They drinks one pint, then sees somebody drink another and make out they be drunk and it's no stronger than cold tay.'

Conversation between these men was of the land. 'How's yer taties, Shepherd?' Jack Fox enquired, knowing full well that the old man's two rows across the headland of Empits were not good.

'Tell tha what, Jack, I've got the finest taters in the Parish, if they was much finer I'm damned if you could see them. I've got some good ones, mind, in the garden helped by the pig muck but the Empits has been ruined by artificial muck. Sulphate and such. I shan't hardly get the seed back.'

The cowman, who liked his beef and lamb, apart from the bacon from his pig, said, 'Is it right that thee bist about to kill a teg this wick, one of them ship feeding on the sprout stems?'

'I'm killing one Friday and the gaffer's selling it to the men. Thurs no trade in the market so put a spoke in for a shoulder or a leg.'

The shepherd chuckled; Jack knew why and whispered to the cowman, 'The Shepherd has the offal when he kills a ship. Well, the liver, the pluck lights, that's his perks mind.'

The two men then bagged up the kibbled cake, the fine meal which fell under the crusher being put in a different bag for the young calves. The shepherd mixed half and half cotton cake with the linseed.

It's a sad reflection on the 1920s that more money could be made from rabbits than from fat tegs or bullocks. The rabbits grazed the hill, it was for free. Every day in the winter Jack's first job in the morning was to visit his rabbit wires and traps on the hill. After dark he and his nephew George walked the rows of snares by the light of a carbide lamp picking up the snared rabbits. Many thousands were caught during the winter months and at one shilling and ten pence a pair that was money in those days.

The shepherd's lambs went to Beckford market in September and were bought in by Arrow and Castle at under a pound a piece. After wintering on the hill the lambs, now tegs, fetched thirty-five shillings each. Frank Moseley gave up sheep farming, some of his old ewes had sold for just five shillings each.

The rather astounding fact is that despire the Depression farmers retained their staff of men, women and boys. Wages were reduced, overtime restricted, but most of the workers in the village worked on the land. Farmers who had grown corn, and cattle and sheep farmers turned to market gardening. The acreage of sprouts Under the Hill increased and spread to the Cotswolds. In years of shortages due to drought, the price in the markets of the north of England was quite good. Of course, there were gluts, but farmers took to growing the relatively new crop. The farmers who had not the labour or the know-how to market the vegetables sold the crop to merchants who picked and marketed the produce themselves. Men who laboured for thirty shillings a week in the summer earned twice that money picking sprouts by the 40 lb pot in winter.

Boys like Arthur Harris went on the land, there was little option. A few found jobs in the local town of Evesham. One family of three sons cycled to town and became lather boys at barber's shops and then hairdressers themselves. One boy was apprenticed to a painter and decorator. The Nortons, Harold and Sapper, were plasterers. Two others worked as errand boys for the Home and Colonial Stores, then elevated to what George Fox called 'counter jumpers' serving in the shop. I reckon that 75 per cent of men and boys were still then employed in full time agriculture.

Although there was mass unemployment in the cities, the situation was not that bad Under the Hill. I saw the tramps plodding the Turnpike Road from one workhouse to the other. The casual wards were full of broken, unemployed men, many of whom had fought in the First World War. A hundred or more of these men and women flocked every summer to the village Under the Hill to work in the pea fields from morning till night. With the money they earned, and peas and potatoes from the fields, they lived rather than existed as they had in the casual wards.

Apart from them, there was an influx of families from Cheltenham. It was their annual holiday, much the same as for the Cockneys who went to Kent for the hop-picking. The families who came were the flower sellers from the Promenade, and odd-job men who did gardening and other jobs for the last of the retired Army families from India. You may well say that surely those sort of people never lived in Cheltenham! The pea-pickers who came from Lower High Street, Grove Street and near the market were a great crowd. There was a community spirit which lifted them. They were industrious folk who would make a living come what may. Some chopped and delivered firewood, others collected potato sacks, selling them at twopence each to market gardeners Under the Hill.

On the hill the late crops of peas thrived nearly one thousand feet up where there was always a breeze. The Lincolns and Senators, famous names of peas, avoided the mildew, a scourge when the heavy dews and fogs came to the vale. Some pickers lived in the barn by the quarry, leaving when the crops finished in October. No peas were picked on Sundays but the farmers Arrow and Castle were keen for the workers to start picking as early as possible on Monday mornings. The men who came as 'Gentlemen of the Road' every year would be picking at first light of morning at four o'clock. Their names often referred to their origins: Scottie, Stafford, Brummie Cock, Manchester.

The hay made from the permanent pasture and the clover of the twenties is so different from the nitrogen-doctored rye grass of today. Alf Blizzard the shepherd liked his ewes to have sweet-smelling hay in winter. When the tractor came to mow the grass, and again to haul it from the fields, he said to me, 'My yows (ewes) won't utt this fodder, it stinks of paraffin from the tractor.' The hill was ranched rather than farmed during the agricultural Depression. Great boar thistles grew on the limestone fields. The walls were not repaired, but the level fields were a picture of red sainfoin blossom in summer and, of course, the peas and sprouts.

The sheep and cattle picked their way through blackberry and hawthorn bushes on the steep slopes. Here again the blackberries were food for free along with the ketchup mushrooms. Summer on the hill was idyllic; it seemed that the air was filled with the sweet twitter of skylarks and the plaintive call of peewits. The clever camouflage of the peewit's nest I remember, the eggs matching the limestone as they lay in a little dent in the field. The birds would cry out when we were near the nest and try to entice us away by settling a distance from their eggs. Partridges would feign a broken wing stumbling along by the stone wall where their nests were situated. One summer I remember a nest shared by the English partridge and the French or Red Legged variety; the hen birds, I think, took the incubating in turn.

Football matches on Saturdays drew quite a crowd because the team was in the first division of the Cheltenham League and had won the Hospital Cup three years running. Nothing hindered the match. Moseley's cows were late for milking; the little Master Men left their holdings to support the team. Albert Hedgecock, the Secretary, carried a collecting box to help with the teams' expenses. He shook the box under Jasper Hill's nose but got no coppers from him. When a charge was made for entry to the ground on a Hospital Cup Final day, Jasper watched the match from the top of his apple tree on the edge of the pitch. When the home team was winning and time was nearly up Fred would kick the ball over the nearby walnut tree. The cry went up 'Keep it on the Island'.

Sundays Under the Hill had a certain feel about them: a sense of funeral when the church bell tolled and life came to a halt. All the children, except those from one family, attended Sunday School at ten o'clock; some went to church, others to chapel. Families were known to switch from the church to the non-conformist or vice versa to qualify for both Sunday School Christmas parties and Sunday School outings in the summer.

Early communion at the church meant a caravan of black-suited gentlemen with their bonneted and veiled ladies passing down the road at five to eight. Parson Butcher shared his bike to get to the church from the next village. He rode half-way, propped the bike against the ash tree at the bottom of Churchway, then his son, Rupert, who had followed on foot, collected the bike and rode the rest of the way to Under the Hill. Rupert overtook his father by Shepherd Blizzard's cottage.

Two worshippers I particularly remember. Old John Yeomans, known as an autocrat, was a bent old man with a demure wife; little Reggie, known as Monkey Brand, a small man with a ginger beard, who walked a few paces behind his enormous wife. He had married late in life to John Yeomans' housekeeper. She was stately dressed in a shot silk affair with lots of lace.

In the fields the horses had a holiday. They seemed to know it was Sunday. At the chapel Sunday School Jim Beckford gave what he called 'topical' lessons. Jim had been a Shepherd, and he talked of The Good Shepherd, but one Sunday he raised the subject of The Bell Wether, a leader of the flock, which carried a bell.

'What was a wether or wedder?' we asked him, and we were told the intricate system of castration.

The village street was quiet apart from Blenheim Hapgood taking Tom Yeomans' cows back to the Lanquet, a little field under the hill. He was so arthritic Blenheim's walk was a perambulation of hob-nailed boots and two ash plants. A few villagers came from Doctor Richardson's with bottles of medicine, bottles wrapped in white paper with dabs of sealing wax closing the joints. 'Don't forget to give it a thundering good shaking before you take it' were the doctor's orders.

Mollie Moseley came from Home Farm with a can of milk for Georgina Coney; Cathie Arrow was taking a can of milk and some eggs to Edie Harris; Bunch Yeomans came from Jack Fox's cottage, where she had been rubbing his back with Wintergreen and liniment for his rheumatism; Henry Richardson was taking a basket of peas to old Albany Hill; Jim Harris was on his way to Percy Harold and Edith Perry with runner beans for their dinner. None of these vegetables were picked on the Sunday. If George Fox forgot to pick the vegetables on the Saturday for Sunday

The church was often a centre of activity in the village

dinner he went without. As Jane Checketts crossed the road to Barbara Cox's house it was obvious she carried something special. They were strawberries enclosed in a rhubarb leaf. Here on Sunday mornings was the social security of the 1920s, a spirit of community.

Some large families with small ovens took their Sunday joints to Albert Checketts' Bake House but few could afford such a luxury. After Sunday dinner some of the older men and women of the land took an afternoon nap. The young families paraded the village street and the lanes, Dad, Mother and children all dressed as well as they could afford. Men in their navy suits, drain-pipe trousers above the ankle showing fancy socks with what was known as 'clock patterns'. The family stopped a while while the men looked over the gates at the crops grown by their neighbours. Some cottagers showed off their pigs in the sties, or their cockerels which would be Christmas dinners. A couple of barrels from a 12-bore gun was a sign that Joe Harris was shooting pigeons in Arrow and Castle's field on the hill. Joe waited in a hide, what he called a cave, and shot the pigeons in the pea field. Sunday or not, the peas had to be protected from pigeons and crows. The ripe strawberries in the Thurness Field were being attacked by hordes of starlings. For three hours after dinner I was there with a Number 3 Garden Gun keeping the birds off the fruit; Ponto had minded them since early morning.

Both church and chapel were full on Sunday evenings and the folk took their pick whether they preferred the intoning of Revd Butcher at the church or the rousing Sankey hymns at chapel. Harry Castle and Tom Arrow were stalwarts at chapel; the Moseleys and Yeomans were worshippers at church. As the chapel people came from the meeting on Sunday night, Tom Arrow's thoughts were on what his men should be working at on Monday morning. No work was done on Arrow and Castle farms on a Sunday except tending the animals, but early on Monday mornings the strawberry pickers were working at first light. George Fox was unofficial foreman and Tom Arrow was anxious to catch him as he came out of chapel to give him the orders for the men for Monday morning. The Sabbath had been observed and even at the Wagon and Horses pub Albert Hedgecock forbade card playing that night.

In 1921 George Moseley presented the village with an Army Hut from the First World War. He paid for it to be erected on his land as a recreation room. A local firm did the building of this early village hall. The men drank so much cider on the building site it took Ponto all his time to carry it from Albert Hedgecock's pub in a bucket. Soon whist drives were held there during the winter months. One stipulation made by the recreation room committee, which was chaired by George Moseley and included Harry Castle and Tom Arrow, was that no intoxicating drink was to be consumed. This did cramp the style of some of the folk, who enjoyed a beer or cider during the interval of the whist drive. Albert Hedgecock solved the problem by hiding bottles of beer under the floor of the room to be consumed at the interval in the orchard. During Lent whist drives ceased altogether.

Despite these restrictions, the recreation room did provide a social centre. A local gentleman gave a full size billiard table for the young men to use. This proved very popular. The ten shillings a week pensioners had their rabbit supper there every Christmas. The church had its parochial tea in the room. Chapel and church Sunday Schools held their Christmas parties there, known as 'Bun Struggles'. All these events in that oil lamp-lit hall depended on one man, Harold Perry. He carried the water for teas from the stand-pipe by the Church; he fired the stove, a coke burning affair which at least warmed a part of the hall.

In the 1920s the village had a Parish Council with five members. It has been said that a parish council is like a calf with its legs tied: it can bawl and do little else. The council Under the Hill did, however, influence both district and county councils, but unsuccessfully opposed the scheme when the village was moved from Gloucestershire into Worcestershire. Perhaps the vestry meeting might have had more success; the Church still kept the village Under the Hill in the Gloucester diocese. One villager who objected to the boundary change commented, 'It's a damn sight warmer in Gloucestershire.' In those days the Vestry meetings were held at ten o'clock in the morning – there were so few rate-payers at that time. Now the parish council and parish meetings are held at 7.30 in the evening.

'If you want to do a bad turn to anyone leave them a thatched cottage in your Will.' These words of Tom Woodcock in the 1920s had a certain ring of truth. Thatching, even then, was expensive and maintenance even more so. Cottages, whether tied ones or not, were rented at three shillings per week, the landlord paying the insurance. If the cottage was a service tenancy the landlord paid rates on it.

Blenheim Hapgood, a bachelor, lived in a thatched cottage and was taken ill. He lived on a pension of ten shillings a week but the Yeoman family helped out by sending him milk and eggs. Tom Arrow who succeeded Dr Richardson as Guardian of the Poor visited him and advised him to apply for assistance from the Relieving Officer. 'I beunt a gwain to be beholden to the Parish. I'll manage,' he replied. After some persuading he was taken to the Relieving Officer and given seven shillings a week.

One often hears the old Poor Law criticized yet with a Guardian in a village it had its merits. You see, the Guardian had his finger on the pulse and knew the conditions of the villagers.

Jasper Hill suffered from lumbago. He went on what was called 'The Box', drawing the standard allowance from the Panel. Someone told Jasper to apply for assistance from the Relieving Officer. At the next meeting of the Board of Guardians the Relieving Officer reported that he had given some relief to Jasper Hill who had said he was destitute.

'Are you sure?' Tom Arrow asked. 'I believe that they have money in the bank, a lot of money. Will you check on that?'

The Relieving Officer visited Jasper and told him that he was led to believe that he had money in the bank. He asked him to declare how much. Jasper was not so thick as folk thought he was.

'No,' he replied, 'If I beunt entitled to Benefit you can have the money back.' To their credit he and his wife had saved several thousand pounds out of very low wages. They had scrimped and saved. Jasper's bike was cleaned every night. It lasted forty years. Real cottage economy.

In 1924 the first council houses were built in the village. Doctor Richardson had at last resigned from the rural district council. His place was taken by Tom Arrow. The doctor, a little man in a frock coat and box hat, had been chairman of the council for many years. He had sat on the minute book to give him more height. The fact that he was stone deaf was a handicap to him and to the council members. It could be quite amusing when the doctor failed to keep up with the proposals.

'Will some one propose the motion?' he would ask.

'Too late, Doctor,' the Clerk would reply. 'It's been proposed and seconded.'

For several years afterwards, the doctor continued to attend to his few patients in the village. Once he sent a bill for forty pounds to Harry Castle for attending to his daughter.

'A lot of money, Doctor. How do you reckon you can charge that amount?'

The doctor replied, 'Ah. But Harry, the drugs I've used are hellishly expensive.'

Harry said, 'If I was lying on that rug dying I wouldn't send for you now.'

The doctor, thinking of no further excuses for the big bill said, 'It's like this, Harry. It's no good me sending bills to patients who haven't got the money.'

When the doctor could no longer practise the old native folk of the village missed him. He had filled in their pension forms, delivered their babies and been such a friend to the poor.

In nature, as in life, nothing stands still. Walt's horses grew older and Tom Arrow with cap reversed and wearing goggles began ploughing with a Fordson Tractor.

Here Under the Hill in the early 1920s life had been peaceful.

By the mid-1920s the honeymoon was over on the farms. The government let the farmers down and the villages Under the Hill turned to market gardening. Blenheim Hapgood declared more than once in the Wagon and Horses, 'This parish stinks of sprouts.' It was true. Corn growing ceased until 1939.

CHAPTER ONE

Two Streams Under the Hill

High on Bredon Hill on an eastern slope is a field known as the Horse Camps. It is here, in a kind of amphitheatre surrounded by a circular moat formation, that the Romans kept their horses during the night. It was vital to guard the animals from wolves or worse in those days.

The hill is a hill of springs; the most prolific run from Paris, a hamlet the other side of Little Hill. At the Horse Camps the two main springs of pure water are about 150 yards apart. We will follow their courses to the River Avon. The interesting point about them is that they join that river via its tributaries at two points ten miles apart.

The first stream runs from the Horse Camps to The Nap, or Knap. Here the land was covered with blackberry bushes, the flat type which produce early fruit similar to the cultivated variety. The hill is steep here, its contour altered in 1926 by a landslip. The hedge to the field below moved about five yards and whether the Knap gained a little is immaterial because the field below, known

1

The mill stream

as Sally Coppice, belonged to the same farmer. The stream fed the water-loving Sallies, or Pussy Willows. Beneath the trees was a carpet of bluebells and primroses in the spring. The stream cascaded over the limestone, and twigs caught up as flotsam and jetsam were fossilized. This stream runs to the west of stream number two and flows on to The Stocking, a ten-acre enclosure which had been a wood, hence its name.

The other stream flowing from the Horse Camps runs along the other side of The Knap, the field on the other side of the hedge being known as The Cow Ground. The big oak tree by the side of the stream was the home of a swarm of bees, the hollow trunk being rich with honey. Past rabbit warrens our stream flows to Van Diemen's Land, a small field with a footpath to a stile and a little stone bridge over the stream. Why Van Diemen's Land? Maybe some Worcestershire chap was transported there. The Stocking is on the west of the stream, still only about 200 yards from stream number one.

The two streams then run roughly parallel and now reach the foot of the hill. Stream number one runs alongside Big Holbrook, a twenty-acre field. Before Arrow and Castle farmed it, the land belonged to a Mr Attwood. He put up a wire fence to keep his cattle out of the stream, which is now called The Holbrook. Using withy posts for the fence they grew and became a line of Withy trees. It is in the field known as Holbrook that a Roman encampment was sited, an obvious place to camp because of the good supply of water and wood. Overlooking the site is Starn Hill.

Stream number two runs the other side of Holbrook, becoming Kersoe Brook. It then runs alongside the Rope Ground, a field which belongs to the church, the rent to be used for buying ropes for the belfry of St Barbara's Church. A bridge over the stream here used to mark the boundary between Gloucestershire and Worcestershire. The Holbrook now crosses the same boundary road, and from then travels alongside Ayles Acre, or Hells Acre, where a dozen or so smallholders scratched a living from that unyielding clay land.

After going under the Saltway at The Roughs Kersoe Brook runs to Furze Hill Farm, where it divides. A part of it becomes The Merry Brook, which joins the River Avon at Charlton. It is used by market gardeners for washing their spring onions and asparagus. The other stream joins the River Isbourne at Hinton near the Mill, then runs on past Narrow Meadow and Hampton Mill, joining the Avon at Battletons Bridge at Hampton.

The Holbrook, after skirting Ayles Acre, runs under the old railway line below Cinder Meadow. The name of this field is interesting – it does not describe what one would think it does. We know that the clay lands were burnt to lighten the soil, producing ash, but Cinder Meadow is a corruption of Set Asunder Meadow, a field asunder from the rest of the farm. After the Holbrook has passed the railway, its course goes through Recked Meadow past Richardson's cow sheds to the main Cheltenham road, where it becomes Carrants Brook. Following the road it passes to The Naits through Catherine's Meadow to The Broadenham, under the Back Lane and through Didcot Ham, to Hill Withy allotment and then crosses the Grafton Lane to Beckford. At the old market it is joined by the Washbourne Brook. It then passes Beckford Inn on its way to Aston on Carrant, through Northway, Newtown and Tewkesbury, where it flows into the River Avon. The Avon soon runs into the Severn at Tewkesbury Hams.

Where the Isbourne joins the Avon at Hampton is many miles from Tewkesbury. Its course is governed by Bredon Hill; flowing through Fladbury, Cropthorne, Pershore, Eckington, Bredon, Twyning to Tewkesbury. It is at Tewkesbury where the two streams of water meet again after coming from so nearly the same source at the Horse Camps on Bredon Hill.

Bredon Hill itself is known for the springing thyme on its hill pastures. Much of the land is now arable but the slopes are still where the thyme grows. Flocks of peewits and larks make music in the springtime. One is never far away from the twittering of the lark as it soars and falls above the barley fields. The lark and the peewit make this hill special.

From Parson's Folly, the tower at the summit of the hill, the vale below is white in April with plum blosson. Shakespeare called it blow, a lovely word still used by the old local gardeners.

Raymond Bush in the 1920s supervized the planting of many thousands of fruit trees on the southern slopes of the hill above Overbury. He was considered an expert on the subject of the spring frosts which kill the blossom. By growing fruit on a higher contour, the blossom will survive the late spring frosts. These frosts settle in the Vale and valleys like water, it's here the damage is done. The fruit trees above Overbury grew some of the finest plums and apples in Worcestershire, the Cox's Orange Pippins were superb. Fruit from Park Farm was renowned for its quality.

Further on round the hill, yet still Under the Hill, lived Walter Martin who was born in 1828 and died in 1919. He was the raiser of the valuable plum which was named after him, Martin's Seedling or Purple Pershore.

He pollinated a Blue Diamond plum tree with a Rivers Early Prolific and sowed the seed in a flower pot. In 1877 he moved to Drakes Broughton three miles from Pershore where he rented ten acres of woodland which he gradually grubbed up, and planted his little plum tree. He grew fruit and vegetables for market and took a great interest in raising apples and plums from their seeds. The Purple Pershore was the best fruit tree he raised. It is a first rate commercial plum and it was grown all over the country when its value became known. Some years ago the original tree still grew at Drakes Broughton. Walter never made a lot of money but was a contented man and in March 1919, he was digging up plum suckers at the age of 91 the day before he died. I knew Walter's widow when she lived with Mr and Mrs Reuben Marshall and was a member of Pershore Baptist Church.

The purple Pershore Plum which Martin raised became one of the most popular plums in the Vale of Evesham. It is slightly tart in taste but when ripe is good for dessert. For canning or bottling it has no equal. What a fine plum Walter gave to Worcestershire.

The little Master Men of the Vale surely gave a lot to market gardening. Mr Spires of Worcester Road, Evesham, introduced The Evesham Wonder Plum. This was a sport from the Pershore

The stream flows gently through this village

Men, boys and their animals pose for a photograph with their reaper binders as they bring the harvest in

Egg Plum, where one branch of the yellow egg produced red plums. Grafts from that tree produced thousands of Evesham Wonder trees years after.

A Mr Crook discovered the Pershore Plum, the yellow egg plum, growing in Tydesley Wood, near Pershore, way back in the nineteenth century. A contemporary of Walter Martin, Rueben Marshall of Pershore experimented in the 1920s by preserving plums in Flowers of Sulphur and marketed what appeared to be fresh plums at Christmas. He collected Peppermint off Bredon Hill and distilled the mint into a cordial which he retailed around the hill villages.

Tom Arrow and Harry Castle planted Pershore Plums, Purple Egg Plums and Evesham Wonder Plums Under the Hill. These varieties owed their existence to Mr Crook, Walter Martin and Mr Spires respectively.

CHAPTER TWO

The Dew Bit

On the day after Boxing Day Arthur Harris, aged fourteen, started work at Manor Farm. His job as plough boy under Walt Chandler was a boy's first job, and Walt himself had started life on the land driving the four horse team many years ago.

Arthur was a handy lad, the youngest of a large family. Walt had been in the army in the First World War. He had been unfortunate, and invalided out of the service, but it was now 1924. The Armistice had not long been celebrated.

Arthur had worked on the farm during his school holidays but now work began in earnest for the boy. Walt wore an Army greatcoat over his corduroy jacket and trousers. Arthur wore an Army tunic cut down quite cleverly by his mother, and although his knees were bare under short trousers his stockings were covered by puttees.

That morning at 6.30 when Arthur arrived at the stable there was no sign of Walt, which was most unusual. Arthur sat on the bench in the gear house where the harness hung ready for the horses. Harry Castle came into the stable. He was one of the farming partners.

'Walt will be here presently, boy. He's cutting a kerf of hay in the rickyard'. Harry added, 'You will be all right with him.'

Walt came into the stable with a square kerf of hay balanced on his head and climbed the ladder into the tallet. The horses were munching their breakfast, a bait of chaff, pulped mangolds and oat flour. From the tallet loft Walt pitched some hay into the racks below. It was sainfoin hay off the hill, smelling as sweet as honey. The horses had almost finished their bait in the manger and all six of them raised their heads to pull wisps of fodder from the racks.

A hurricane lantern hung from a plough's traces at the foot of the ladder, another gave shadows that winter morning from the gear house.

'You had no cause to get yer afore seven, Arthur, but being as youm here give the hosses a bowl full each of the corn out of the bin.'

Arthur opened the metal corn bin and scooped some corn for the teams. The clank of the metal lid caused all the horses to turn around and look at the boy. They knew where the tasty corn was kept, and young Arthur gave a bowl full to each of the six horses in the stable.

By 7.15 Walt Chandler had geared up four of his horses, Turpin and Boxer, sons of Flower, who was also in the team that morning, and the ridge-backed gelding Captain.

'We be gwain to start ploughing the stubble in Thurness, thurs twenty acres of clay there so we shan't want another job for a while. Come on, bwoy, let's give you a leg up onto Turpin. Thee hast ridden him afore in the hayfield.'

Arthur rode the foremost horse in the team, followed by Flower, Boxer and old Captain, Walt walked in a nautical roll behind, using a plough paddle as a walking stick, and to clear the plough mould-board and share of clay. His frail basket hung from Turpin's hames along with Arthur's little straw frail basket.

It was still only partly light as the little caravan of horses, man and boy made their way to the Thurness field. Walt clicked his tongue and the team quickened their pace. The three horses in front of Captain were in long gears, trace horse harness. Between Turpin and Flower a wooden spreader kept the traces apart, another spreader fitted between larger links in the chain harness did likewise. Captain, apart from his trace harness, wore a cart saddle, a ridge chain between the traces fitting into the grooves of the saddle to keep the traces at the right height. Captain's traces were hooked onto the front of the plough, known as the hake.

'Now then.' Walt spoke to Arthur. 'This is a fresh job for thee, bwoy. See that young ash tree in the hedge on the adlund (headland). Lead Turpin straight for there.' Walt was doing a job he had done for thirty years but Arthur was his new plough boy.

The plough bit into the stubble and turned a shallow furrow of clay until the headland was reached. Arthur turned the team on the headland and Walt told him to steer for a blackthorn on the other headland. A bed had now been marked out, and the team had to follow the open furrow and cast the bed.

'Now then, bwoy, thee hast got that new whip on the hames from Ernie at Beckford and I know that you can crack it. No hitting the 'osses mind, the weals will show up on their hips and I'll get the blame. When Boxer is lagging, just speak to him – cup, cup – and crack the whip.'

The four horses stepped along the furrow, Turpin the foremost, Flower the lash horse, Boxer the body horse and Captain the filler. At the bottom headland Walt called, 'Turn Jinkum' to turn them to the right. At the top headland he called 'Turn come again', turning to the left. The clay land stuck lovingly to the boots of man and boy. It lay from the furrow like rashers of bacon joined together from headland to headland.

'It 'ull want some frost to lax this lot,' Walt observed as he cleaned some of the sticky clay from his boots on the iron frame of the plough.

By ten o'clock the train had left the branch line station and the work was pleasing Walt. A part of a bed of land now brown steamed under a weak sun. Walt liked the way the ploughing lay like a well-dug garden.

As the team reached the headland Walt called 'Whoa!' He put a corn sack over each of the steaming horses and said to Arthur, ''Tis bait time and I'm ready for some fittle as I only had a dew bit this morning.'

Arthur had heard the expression used by his father many times so he understood Walt. It's a bit of food eaten early in the morning while the dew is still on the grass.

'Let's get on the burra side of the hedge. It's a coldish wind. What ast got for thee bait, Arthur?'

Man and boy sat under the thick blackthorn hedge in the Thurness field. Arthur took his bait from his frail basket and said, 'Look yer, Walt, what dost think of that for bread pudding? Our Mam made it yesterday.'

'Her's a good woman, Mrs Harris, and thee bist the best one of her younger bwoys.'

Walt took out of his basket the top of a cottage loaf, a piece of cheese and a large purple Tripoli onion grown in his garden. He then took the cork from his quart bottle and took a swig of cold tea. As he drank his Adam's apple went up and down like a plum bob. The faded label on the bottle had the legend 'Vat 69'. His frail was a do-it-yourself workshop, for it contained all the things needed for temporary mending of the plough and the harness: shut links to mend the plough traces, horse nail stubs to fix spreaders, cart nails for cleats to hold the plough wheels, leather thongs called thunks to repair harness, a heavy plough spanner and some whip cord.

Arthur's father, Jim Harris, worked as carter on Home Farm. He was second man to the head carter Jack Chapel. Jack was an old man and had been a cruel one with boys and horses. His horses often had shown the wheal marks on their flanks which Walt avoided. He used to throw clats, or lumps of clay, at his plough boys. In temper he smashed the cogs on the binder when he could not make it work. This was during the hot summer of 1921. The ground was cracked, or chauned, and the pieces of the cog wheel fell down the chauns. He said in his temper that they had gone to Australia when his employer arrived and sent him away from the harvest field to take three horses and some Duckfeet Drags (heavy harrows) and cultivate a fallow field. It was then that Arthur's father Jim was given the job of harvesting the wheat with a binder. Jim Harris was a quiet, peaceable man. He looked after the horses well and was an expert in breaking in the cart colts.

Shire horses being paraded in full dress harness at a local show

A young farmer's lad leads the team of oxen as they plough

12

'What's thee Dad doing today? Is he gone to plough? Master George Moseley's 'osses looks better now yer Dad sees to them. Old Jack was cruel. I've heard of some of his lapses.'

Arthur replied, 'Our Dad's walking half way to Brumijum (Birmingham) today along of one of his best mares, named Violet. He 'unt very pleased with parting with her. Another of Master Moseley's 'osses 'as bin pulling the heavy drays on the streets of Brumijum and has got bad feet through pulling heavy loads on the stone sets in the city. The carter from Brum is meeting our Dad half-way and he's swapping over his 'oss with Violet, and Dad is bringing the lame 'oss to Home Farm.'

Walt took a lump of cheese and cut it with his knife and remarked, 'This cheese is as hard as the Devil's back teeth. I'll tell Master Allin's outright representative what I think of it when he comes Friday night. I know how your Dad feels over Violet. The Army took the best 'osses from the farms during the First World War, and the carter shed some tears, I can tell ya.'

Walt lit his pipe and the smell of the Red Bell tobacco wafted to Arthur who said, 'Our Uncle Job smokes twist and chews it. You should see how far he spits across the room into the fire.'

Walt replied, 'They got a spittoon at the pub for some of the old boys. I reckon 'tis not nice.'

Arthur started to laugh. Walt asked, 'What bis't laughing at, summat I said?'

Arthur was thinking of his Uncle Job and told Walt that on Sunday he had complained that he had no twist tobacco to chew, Arthur had picked up what he thought to be twist and gave it to old Job to chew, but it was where the cat had excused himself on the couch.

'Oi, bwoy! Job had a hard time as a bwoy and so did I. I was hired out on a farm on the Cotswolds and had to sleep in a bothy above the kitchen. The farmer wouldn't let me have a candle to go to bed, and I groped my way to bed in the dark. What dos't think I had for breakfast?' Arthur shook his head.

'Cider sop – bread soaked in cider. I was thirteen, but I'll never forget it.'

Walt rose to his feet and said, 'Come on, bwoy. We can't do too much for a good master.'

The four horses, driven by Arthur, stepped out down the furrow. Arthur showed the carter that he could crack the whip. The clay land was so heavy that Walt was able to loose the plough tails and walk with his plough boy beside the team.

'When you turn on the adlund, just watch that Captain doesn't run off out of the furrow. We shall have a furrow like a dog's hind leg, else.'

At three o'clock Walt hooked his team from the plough and man and boy and horses went up the road half a mile to the stable. Walt sat side-saddle on Boxer, his favourite chestnut gelding. While Walt ungeared his team and hung the harness on the pegs in the gear house, Arthur with a withy skip, or hamper, partly filled the manger with the horses' dinner – chaff, mangolds, oat flour and bean flour. As he stood by the corn bin, Walt called to him from the gear house, 'Now then, look sharp and throw some fodder down into their racks from the tallet.'

Arthur climbed the ladder and filled the hay racks with sweet hay, sainfoin.

'After dinner we be gwain to fetch a load of fother (fodder) on a muck cart with Blackbird and pitch it into the tallet, and I want you to clean the stable out. I shan't turn the 'osses out into the Close till half-past five.'

After dinner, man and boy did what Walt had planned. At tea-time Arthur's dad, Jim Harris, came in tired after walking half-way to Birmingham and back.

At the back of their cottage the Harris garden backed onto some woodland where George Moseley's gamekeeper reared pheasants. Arthur was proud as a boy would be at fourteen of the way he could crack a whip. He took his whip into the garden and cracked it for half-an-hour. The sound echoed around the wood. The gamekeeper, who had been troubled with poachers, came into the Harris's garden thinking that someone was shooting at his birds with a gun.

On Friday night Tom Arrow paid the men. Walt Chandler's

wage was thirty-two shillings and Arthur's nine shillings for fifty-two hours. Mrs Harris, Arthur's mother, gave him sixpence pocket money. He delivered the *Evening Echo* to subsidize his little pocket money.

The boys in the village who had left school met at Binnie's. There were two things that appealed to them on those cold winter nights: first, she had a good open fire, as her brother kept her supplied with coal and logs; secondly, she had a gramophone. In those pre-wireless days a gramophone was something special. The boys clubbed together and bought records when they had the money. One tune that could be heard from her cottage was 'When Father painted the Parlour'. Then she bought a dartboard and her son, Bill, fetched a jar of cider from the pub opposite. It was at Binnie's that Arthur smoked his first Woodbine cigarette.

Ned was plough-boy for George Moseley on the Home Farm. It was said that he was three half-pence short of a shilling, but he was a good lad to work either under Jack Chapel or Jim Harris. He went to Binnie's club. Ned never learned to read or write and Arthur used to read to him from the *Echo*.

Perhaps some of the things missing in the countryside today are sounds long since gone. The clip clop of heavy horses up and down the village street, the jingle of chain harness, the creak of wagons and the sound of hob-nailed boots. Arthur used to scuff his nailed boots as he walked down the village street to Binnie's and he watched the sparks fly as the metal hob nails struck the stones. The story is that when Ned bought his first pair of hob-nailed boots he forgot to cut the string which tied them together and he walked part of the way from the station with them tied. He was a boy of the land and studied the birds and flowers. Living with his grandparents, no doubt some of his ways had rubbed off them. 'Yer look!' he said one day, 'The crows be cider making in the sky. We shall get some tempest (thunder).'

It took Walter and Arthur a month to plough The Thurness and then they were pea-planting in Finches Piece.

CHAPTER THREE

Fred Chapel and the Cattle Plague

On Saturday, 11 November, 1924 a football match was held in The Wynch. It was no ordinary match but a round in The Hospital Cup. Hundreds of folk came by bike, motor bike, horse and trap, while some walked.

That afternoon Fred Chapel, cowman to Arrow and Castle, drove twenty shorthorn cows up the lane for milking. Blenheim Hapgood followed with Frank Moseley's herd.

When the cows had been tied up in the cowshed, Fred noticed that four of them just snorted on the cattle cake in the manger. On examination Fred saw that their mouths and noses were sore and running with mucus. Every now and again the cows licked furiously at their feet, which were inflamed. The cows were slightly lame. Young Frank Harris, Arthur's brother, was under-cowman. Fred Chapel told him, 'Thee go and fetch the gaffer, thurs something radically wrong with these cows.'

Tom Arrow came across the yard and found the cowman looking very upset. Fred said, 'These cows won't eat their fittle and their feet be sore and they slobbers at the mouth.'

Heavy threshing tackle had to be hauled into position by four sturdy horses

A man with a milking pail in a field of Jersey cows

There being no telephone in the village, Tom Arrow drove his cob and governess cart to fetch the vet. It looked like foot-and-mouth disease, so the vet ordered the cows to be left in their stalls overnight until the disease could be confirmed the next day.

Fred fed the animals that evening and the old man spent the first part of the night with the hurricane lamp looking round his little, precious, herd.

The next day the Ministry vet ordered all the cows and calves to be slaughtered. Fred Chapel remembered when Squire Yeoman's cattle had had the disease years ago and young Joe Yeoman had fed the cows on oatmeal slop and most had survived.

Monday morning Walt Chandler took a horse and dray to the station to get some coal. The animals were to be burned. Arthur and Frank Harris went with another dray to Syd Checketts, the baker, for some ash faggots to start the fire. When Walt Chandler arrived with the coal he fetched some paraffin and some straw. The slaughtermen arrived while Fred Chapel was saying his goodbyes to the cows. Spot, a red shorthorn who was giving six gallons of milk a day, was in another shed with Grannie, a pure bred Hereford cow and the mother of the stock bull. Fred met the men with their humane killers and said, 'You chaps an't a gwain to kill the two in the loose box. They bain't infected. Spot's the babby's cow, Mrs Arrow reared her second bwoy on her milk.'

'Our orders be to slaughter the lot. I see the fire's all laid. We shall start after lunch.'

Frank Harris was sixteen but he looked upon the cowman as a father. When the milking was finished, Fred used to play tunes on his tin whistle and on summer evenings in the garden of his cottage his concertina could be heard playing Sankey hymns.

Walt Chandler chose Turpin as trace horse to drag the dead cows to the fire. As the cows were shot in turn the next to be killed halted on the brink of the execution. They smelled death. Turpin did not enjoy his part of the affair. To drag cows' carcases to the fire caused Turpin to jib.

The time came for Spot to be killed. Fred Chapel had pleaded in vain.

'I can't stop yer, thee look after things, Frank,' he said to young Harris. Across the yard the cowman walked to Tom Arrow's back door. Tears were streaming down his unshaven face, he had had two sleepless nights.

'I can't stop yer and see this lot, Master.' He spoke between his tears.

'All right, Fred, we understand. You go home for a couple of days,' Tom Arrow replied.

There would be no cows to milk and Fred Chapel was a stockman. He was a broken man and he never returned to the farm. He could be seen in the mornings the following summer sitting under his plum tree playing his concertina and singing 'Dare to be a Daniel, Dare to stand alone.' Fred stood alone but died in the autumn. As for Walt Chandler, he said that it was weeks before he could get rid of the smell of burnt cattle. The fire's flames rose high above the hedges that November night.

It seems strange, but Frank Moseley's cows never contracted the disease although they had followed Fred Chapel and his herd down the lane. After a time Arrow and Castle bought more milking cows, but they were never a patch on Fred Chapel's herd which had contracted foot-and-mouth that Armistice day.

CHAPTER FOUR

'Good Hay Hath no Fellow'

This saying is so true today when less and less of our pastures are mown for hay now that silage is valuable fodder for winter. Shakespeare, who lived a part of his life alongside the Avon meadows, wrote, 'Rarely smells the new mown hay.' When hay matured in the rick and not in the bale, the hay knife cutting through the packed herbage released the smell of summer on the coldest winter's day.

Walt Chandler, when mowing the brookside meadows in the 1920s, started a job which took twelve men and boys to complete in ricking the hay. This spare little man with arched eyebrows, which gave him a surprised look, rose at 3.30 a.m. on those June mornings, ready to start work at four o'clock. His cottage home was way up on a hill overlooking the Cotswolds. Mr Avens, a city business man had a weekend cottage near Walter. He provided him with cast-off clothes. Mr Avens being a fairly tall man, his trousers were much too big for Walt. Nevertheless Walt wore them and they reached well above his waist up under his armpits;

it meant that Walt needed no waistcoat and that little of his shirt was visible. Mr Avens also gave Walt a pair of cast-off plus-fours, which he wore on bell ringing nights.

The meadows near the brook were heavy with dew in the early morning. One field, known as The Dewrest, told it all lying beside two narrow meadows called The Needle Lands. Walt's mowing machine chattered around The Dewrest, the agitating knife cutting the trefoil, clover, cornflower, meadowsweet and all the herbs which grow in old pasture. Mole hills, which Walt called oonty tumps, would clog the knife of the machine but soon flocks of starlings and other birds settled on the newly mown swath. They were after the worms and insects exposed by Walt's machine. At six o'clock Arthur Harris arrived with a rake to what was known as 'rake the back swath' – the swath nearest to the hedge was raked back to enable another swath to be cut under the hedge by circling the field the opposite way round. Walt produced a file and told Arthur to sharpen another knife for the machine. He did this and Walt put the sharpened knife on the machine, telling Arthur to sharpen the blunt one. By ten o'clock the flies and horse flies, known as old maids, were worrying the horses, Walt had laced elderberry blossoms in the bridles to discourage them. By half-past ten half the field had been mown. Walt unhooked his pair of horses from the mower and man and boy had their morning bait in the shade, then they took the horses to the stable at Manor Farm.

Harry Castle met them saying, 'I suppose it's too hot for mowing now, Walt.'

The carter raised his eyebrows and replied, 'Hot! It's too hot for my 'osses and the old maids by the brook torments um. I'll take another couple of 'osses ater tay and finish the grounds when them blood-suckers be gone.'

Harry Castle said, 'Take this boy with you and Tom the nag and horse-hoe the sprouts the rest of the day.'

Man and boy horse-hoed between the sprout rows, Walt holding the horse hoe and Arthur leading Tom the nag. When the sun went down Walt finished mowing The Dewrest. Then he walked up the hill with a couple of loaves from Albert Checketts the Baker, who gave him a pint of cider. At his cottage Clara, his wife, had a meal ready of boiled bacon, broad beans and potatoes.

After a pipe of tobacco Walt said, 'I'm going up the wooden hill and shan't need any rocking before I'm asleep. It's ten o'clock and the alarm ull go off at half-past three in the morning. I suppose we got to make hay while the sun shines.'

Next day Arthur was sent with the swath-turner to turn the green hay. Harry Castle put his trap pony Molly between the shafts of the turner. Walt was mowing in the next field, The Needle Lands.

'Now thee be careful with that young mare of the gaffer's. His wife thinks the world of her. She's fast in the trap, so just thee be careful.'

Arthur thought himself a hell of a fellow riding on the swath-turner, steering Molly with the rope reins known as 'G. O. Lines'. He sat alongside Walt for dinner in the shade. Walt asked, 'How much of the field have you turned, 'cos the gaffer expects it to be finished afore night.'

'I'll finish it, don't worry, Walt, if it's moonlight. It's nice riding after all that walking ploughing and harrowing.'

'So you might think bwoy, my ass is as sore as a boil.'

After dinner, when the sun was hot, Molly was half-walking half-trotting round the field when the rake disturbed a wasp's nest and the wasps attacked mare and boy. Molly ran as fast as she did when pulling the trap and Arthur fell from the rake. Molly stopped by the hedge over which Walt was mowing. Arthur was in tears. Walt held Molly and nothing was broken.

'What bist whimpering for bwoy? Nothing is broken.'

Arthur gasped between his tears, 'What ull Mrs Castle say?'

Walt laughed and said, 'Not thy fault, it's they warm assed wops.'

By next day the hot sun had turned the swathes from green herbage into sweet-smelling hay. The clover in the mixture, which had been in red bloom, was now a delicate fawn colour; wild yellow trefoil had wilted under the hot June sun. The smell of the mixture was so idyllic.

Arthur was now putting four swathes into one row, known as a window or walley. As the hay was moved the stubble revealed thousands of insects, food for the starlings. As the gulls and rooks followed the plough for worms, so the starlings fed on the myriad of insects and ant eggs. A partridge had been killed by Walt's mower and the eggs she was sitting on taken to Tom Arrow, who put them under a broody hen. He had done the same thing the year before but the chicks had been taken by a rat. By afternoon the hay was fit to rick. The long rows were just the width for the broad-wheeled wagon to go between. The hay crackled and a sudden whirlwind took a wisp up high in the sky. Arthur marvelled, but the men took that as a sign of thunder.

Walt Chandler had made a staddle in the rickyard of Manor Farm. He had used some loose straw and a little load of mouldy hay from the year before; it was the foundation of the rick, carefully stepped out in a rectangle ten yards long and five yards wide. Tom Arrow and Tom Woodcock built the ricks with Alf Blizzard, while Frank Harris and Jim Harris unloaded the wagons in turn.

It was about half a mile from the brookside meadow, The Dewrest, to Harry Castle's rickyard at Manor Farm. Harry always worked in the hayfield so that one of the partners was in the rick yard and the other in the hay field. He had as hay-pitchers George Fox and Fred Woodcock, while Jack Fox, George's uncle, stood on the load and loaded the wagons. Harry Castle was in charge. He organized the loads and saw that they were roped when they left the field.

Old Ponto, who lived and slept in the granary was an odd character only fit to do boys' jobs. He lead the horses in the field between the walleys and shouted 'hold tight' or 'hold fast' to Jack on the load. The weather being fine meant that Walt was mowing another field. That morning Walt had taken two four-wheeled wagons into The Dewrest meadow ready for loading with hay. After dinner Arthur took another wagon to the field with Flower in the shafts and Turpin as trace horse. George, Fred, Jack and Ponto rode down in another wagon with Captain in the shafts.

Two horses pull a well-loaded hay wagon

Rick-thatchers at work on Mile End Farm

This wagon was loaded first of all, Ponto leading the horse between the rows of hay.

Jack Fox had been working on the farm since the squire's time; he was a handy man who could mend or make wagon shafts or ladders. His problem was his love of cider and when he had been drinking Tom Arrow said he could be 'conterary' (contrary). He took the hay from the two pitchers, one either side, and filled the bed of the wagon working with his own short shuppick (sheaf pike) or hay fork. Fred and George pitched the hay with long forks, the long handles of which they called stales and the prongs, grains. The language of the hayfield remained unaltered in the 1920s from the days of Queen Victoria. Village and country life was still uncontaminated by the town let alone American television and the radio. After the bed of the wagon had been filled, George said to his Uncle Jack, 'Where dost want this pitch-full?'

'Corners on the back,' came the reply.

George placed his pitch-full on the back corner of the wagon on his side. Fred put his pitch-full on the other side.

'Hold tight,' shouted Ponto and Captain snatched forward.

Jack called out, 'Mind what thee bist at letting that 'oss snatch so. Thee ull have me ass over yud else.'

Ponto picked up a little hay to feed the horse.

'Where dost want this pitch-full?' George called to Jack.

Here the language of the hayfield was still foreign to the outsider. Jack replied, 'Plant wad.' George, knowing of old where to put the hay, placed his pitch-full in front of the one on the corner to bind it. Fred asked Jack where to place his pitch-full and Jack said, 'Egarn wad,' and he bound his corner. The same system applied to the front corners, etc.

Then, as George called, 'Where dost want this pitch-full? tis only as big as a crow's nest the hay is so slick (slippery to pitch)?' Jack replied, 'In the middle under my fit.'

When the load was done, Arthur hitched Turpin to the front of Captain as the trace horse. The load was then roped, and Arthur took it up Gipsies Lane toward Manor Farm.

'Mind that gate post when thee goes into the lane.' George

called. Arthur had a leading rein on Turpin and led Captain through the gateway. Up the lane the wagon rocked and rolled over the rough limestone track. The overgrown hedges combed the side of the load so that wisps of hay decorated the lane.

In Manor Farm rickyard Frank Harris met his brother and lead Turpin up the slope drawing the wagon, with Captain in the shafts and Arthur leading him alongside the staddle.

It was easy for Frank Harris to unload the first few loads on to the staddle as he pitched the hay down to the rick-builders. As the wagons were unloaded young Arthur took them to the hayfield and returned with a full load. On the hot June day everything went like clockwork. If the hay-pitchers had a load ready and Arthur was not back with the empty wagon, old Ponto took the load as far as the gateway. Ponto could be a difficult man but Fred, George and Jack knew how to handle him.

It was a fact in the village that if things went wrong Ponto was blamed. Phil Richardson, the doctor's son, had a donkey which fell into the parish quarry and broke its back. Ponto was blamed: the lads in the village said that he had pushed the donkey over the side of the quarry. Jack Yeoman's pig choked himself and Ponto was called 'choke pig'. To see Ponto chasing the lads in the village street on sumer nights when they teased him was sad. Ponto had been crossed in love and was an odd character. He was very suspicious and had cause to be. Tom Arrow tried to look after him. In the First World War Ponto used to eat all his rations in a couple of days and then kick at the door of Albert Checketts' shop demanding more rations. There could have been a tragedy one summer night when the lads told Ponto that the Devil was in the churchyard in some ivy by an old gravestone. Ponto took an axe from Jack Fox's workshop and went up to the churchyard. Young Harold Norton had been hiding in the ivy. Ponto swung the axe at the ivy, but fortunately Harold had moved away in time. Ponto was happy in the hayfield and so fond of the horses he fed them hay from the walley as the men pitched the hay.

Up in the rickyard at Manor Farm as the rick got higher than the wagon-loads, Tom Arrow decided to erect the elevator pole, known as the monkey pole. A pole supported by four guy ropes had a jib attached and to the jib, suspended by a rope through the pulley at the end of the jib, some forks were attached. The other end of the rope went alongside the rick to a trace horse; when the horse was backed, the swinging jib let the forks go onto the load of hay alongside. The unloader put the forks into the hay and when the horse went forward the jib swung over the rick as the hay was elevated: a very efficient, easy mechanical contraption for unloading hay.

No hay has ever been baled and smelt as sweet as the June hay in Tom Arrow and Harry Castle's rickyard. The roof was put on the rick and when it settled topped up with more hay. In a couple of weeks all the ricks were ready for thatching. Tom Harris, Jim Harris's cousin, thatched all the ricks in the village. He was also a good house thatcher but every year he reckoned to be rick thatching in August.

Tom was a strong man who had fought the Turks in Salonika and emigrated to Canada, but as his wife never followed him he returned. Tom was a man not to argue with. One chap who had left the village and come back one weekend said the village chaps were swede-gnawers. Tom took him outside and gave him the hiding of his life, saying 'I'll show you whether I'm a swede-gnawer or not.'

Tom spoke in riddles, never finishing a sentence. He would say 'You understand my meaning' (we never did), 'That's a very funny thing' or 'There you are' and he was always saying 'I turned round.' He kept a pig for himself that lived in a sty next to where he had his cider. He was nonplussed one day as he described the pig being choosey over its food: 'I cut some cabbages in the garden, put them in my barrow, turned round and took the cabbages to the pig and turned round, and do you know that pig turned round and wouldn't eat it. So I turned round and took the cabbages back down the garden.'

Tom is remembered most of all by the parade of the British Legion on Armistice Day. Tom wore a bowler hat and navy suit. His medals hung from his lapel like a martingale on a cart-horse.

He marched better than most of the men. Sadly he is with us no more. No more shall we hear Tom sing his songs as at the Armistice tea when his voice rang out those well-known words, 'The beautiful picture in the beautiful golden frame' and 'If those lips could only speak'.

CHAPTER FIVE

The Squire

Both Jim Harris, who worked for George Moseley, and Walt Chandler, who worked for Tom Arrow and Harry Castle, as young chaps worked for the Squire. They remembered the scene at Manor Farm thirty years ago when Jim Arrow came back to the village on holiday and these three men talked of the old times. Jim Arrow was the one who got away! He left the village about 1895 to work on the Midland Railway.

To say that Squire Yeomans was eccentric is putting it mildly; his life had taken on the style of Rip Van Winkle. It was as if he had arrived in the nineteenth century after a hundred years of sleep. He even kept 6 January as Christmas Day – the Christmas Day of the old calendar.

The scene was Manor Farm rickyard. The squire's steam engine was threshing wheat. Every sack weighed $2\frac{1}{4}$ cwt. The threshing gang apart from Jim Arrow and Jim Harris were old crippled men; some came to work on two sticks, crippled with arthritis. The two Jims were carrying the sacks from the thresher up some steps into the granary. By knocking-off time at five o'clock the two men were too tired to eat their tea. Jim Arrow thought that that night he would have it out with the Squire.

29

'Look here, Sir,' he began, 'Harris and I are doing all the hard work. I want more money. Ten shillings a week is no good to me.'

The Squire asked, 'Why?'

Jim replied, 'You've got all these old men hobbling about on sticks and they get the same wage as me.'

The Squire said, 'Ah, but I had the best out of them and now I'll have the worst.'

In the 1890s the Squire was one of the few ratepayers in the village. The Rates were agreed at the vestry meeting. They were spent on the roads and on maintenance of the workhouse. Some had Parish Relief of two shillings and sixpence a week paid for out of the Rates. The Squire knew that if he didn't find the old men a job he would, in the main, be paying for their Parish Relief.

'I'll make a deal with you, young fella. I shan't pay you more wages, you are getting more than you deserve already.'

Jim Arrow wondered what the deal would be. The Squire took one hundred golden sovereigns from his pocket and showed the coins to Jim. 'You would like that lot young fella?' the Squire said teasingly. Then came the crunch. Offering Jim his gun and some cartridges he said, 'There's a hundred sovereigns for you on condition you take this gun and cartridges and shoot Doctor Richardson.'

Jim packed his bag that week and took a job on the railway in Leicestershire.

The Squire got more and more dangerous with his gun. When Jim was a boy he had had to go with him shooting at owls on the hill at night. Gipsies Lane was and is a crooked lane. One winter the Squire took Jim Harris, Walt Chandler, Jack Chapel and Blenheim Hapgood down the lane and ordered them to straighten it. 'Any man who doesn't make the lane dead straight with pick and shovel I'll shoot,' he said.

He stood there until he could see that, owing to the roadside ditch, it was impossible to straighten the lane. There is a stretch where it is straight today, perhaps that's where the men were successful!

With a shot-gun tucked under his arm Mr Charles Blackwell poses outside Church Farm

31

The Squire became so trigger-happy that the keeper or male nurse who came to look after him took the shot out of his cartridges.

Jim Harris as a young chap had lots of stories about the Squire.

'There, young fella,' he said to Jim one day. 'I want thee to taste the cider in the barn.' There in the thatched barn barrels and barrels of cider were in a row under the wall. The Squire drew half a pint from the first barrel. 'What's that like Jim?' he asked.

'Pretty good, Gaffer,' he replied.

He drew some from the next barrel. 'How does that taste, young fella?'

'Not quite so good, Gaffer.' The next was said to be better; but by the time Jim had sampled cider out of each barrel he just didn't know what to say, for by then he had got past knowing or caring whether the cider was good or bad.

It seemed that no one who worked for the Squire escaped some of his mad schemes. Blenheim Hapgood was cowman. He had plenty of cider allowed him and for Sunday morning's work he breakfasted on eggs and boiled bacon. He grew potatoes on the headland of the corn field and survived on ten shillings a week. As he turned the cows out of their stalls one morning, the Squire was in the orchard feeding the hens and the ducks.

He called to Blenheim, 'I want you for a few minutes.'

'What is it, Gaffer?' Blenheim asked.

'See those ducks, they are shovelling the corn up and the hens are picking it up.'

'Oi, I suppose they be.' Now what's he going to do, Blenheim wondered.

'Catch that drake,' the Squire ordered.

Blenheim caught the drake and the Squire took a penknife from his pocket and sharpened the drake's bill, threw the bird on the ground, and said, 'Now pick up the same as the hens.'

Blenheim said nothing, it didn't do to!

Walt Chandler as a boy worked under a carter called Nailus, short I suppose for Cornelius. The half-gallon of cider the Squire allowed his men was ample for most of the workers, but Nailus drank the lot before bait time.

Walt told the story of finding the Squire sitting in a wheel-barrow in the middle of the Moat Pond and saying that he was fed up with England and he was off to America.

The Squire used to attend the local markets and if he wanted to buy horses, cattle or any other stock he would pay over their value. Local farmers knew this and they and the dealers would run the Squire up to ridiculous prices. Walt said that he bought horses for a pastime. 'He bought scores of cart-'osses ten years old and never been broken. Nailus and me just gave um fittle in the winter, but who could handle a 'oss ten year old and never broken?'

It is a fact that folks will cling round anyone free with their money like bees around a honey pot. Yes, the Squire had his so-called friends who helped him to spend his money. He told Blenheim Hapgood one summer's day to catch four drakes off the duck pond and bring them into his big kitchen. 'I've got some friends coming today and we are going to have some sport.'

Blenheim did as he was told, leaving the drakes in a crate in the kitchen.

'Fetch the big bath from the washhouse,' he told Blenheim. Blenheim fetched the bath and half-filled it with port.

'Here, have a glass, Blenheim,' the Squire said.

'I bain't used to strong liquor, Gaffer.'

Four local fellows arrived, including the estate carpenter. Blenheim was ordered to put the drakes into the bath of port. The Squire then got the men to bet on the drakes as they swam from one end of the bath to the other.

'You have never seen duck races, Blenheim?'

'No, Gaffer, but it seems a waste of good drink – I relished the glass you gave me.'

'You will have more later if you do as I say,' the Squire said.

The Squire, the estate carpenter, and his three other farmer guests then played cards and drank whisky all day. Blenheim took the drakes back to the pond.

At Simonds Brewery the head of a cask is being made smooth with a topping plane

Blenheim, Jim Harris, his brother Job, Jack Fox, Jack Chapel and others were called into the kitchen at the Manor that evening and invited to drink the port from the bath. Needless to say, they got blind drunk and spent the night in the Squire's kitchen.

One frosty morning the Squire came into the yard followed by the usual pack of dogs. They were all breeds, all sizes, Airedales, spaniels and a lurcher named Brindy.

'Jim,' he said to Jim Harris, 'these dogs are starved to death. Fetch them some cider.'

Jim fetched a bottle of the cider he was allowed from the stable.

'Give them some cider.'

Jim poured cider into their mouths, some went in one side and out the other. He gave each of them some except the old lurcher Brindy.

'What about Brindy, Jim? You afraid of him?'

'I be, Gaffer. I be mortally afraid of that lurcher, he ud as leif bite one as look at me, and besides, Gaffer, they have drunk nearly all my cider.'

The Squire had had his joke and laughingly told Jim to go and fill his bottle up in the barn.

No doubt that the Squire was more of a knave than a fool. He was accepted well, he had to be by the working folks. Jasper Hill, the coalman, who worked for Taylors at the station wharf called on the Squire who bought his coal by the truck-load. 'Can I sell you a truck load of coal, Gaffer?' Jasper inquired.

'No, I don't want any more. We had to burn the last lot,' came the reply.

Jasper, who related the story in one of the rare times he visited the Star Inn, said, 'I don't know what you chaps thinks of that, but that's the honest truth and as Jack Fox says "the truth needs no study".'

Jack Fox remembered a time way back in the 1860s when the railway line connecting the village with Birmingham was opened. The Squire gave a dinner on that occasion to the men and women of the village. He travelled on the train in those days and on inquiring how long the next train would be, a cheeky porter replied, 'Now quite as long as the platform, Sir.' The porter was reported and was disciplined.

It was twenty years later that the Squire became a recluse; for two years no one saw him and he remained hiding in the Manor. One day in the winter the Squire's men were threshing a rick of wheat. It was dinner time and the gang were sitting in the barn nearby eating their meal. It gave fireman Davis the engine driver a shock when the Squire arrived. His engine lay still in the rickyard.

'Get them wheels a moving, Fireman,' he said sharply. The men didn't move, but Davis climbed on his engine, opened the throttle valve, and the driving belt from the flywheel turned the threshing drums, giving the well known tune 'More, more, more'. The engine was only at half-throttle, the threshing machine turned quite slowly and no one fed any sheaves into the drum, but for the Squire to see one of his 'black 'osses', as he called his steam engines, working satisfied him.

His two years as a recluse were over and at a later date another rick was being threshed. As was the custom a woman stood on the engine and cut the string bands from the sheaves, the engine driver fed the sheaves into the drum. The Squire arrived at bait time and looked at the wheat in the sacks. Mrs Dance said to him, 'It's a good sample, Squire.'

'Yes it is,' he replied, 'and if you can carry a sack to your cottage you can keep it.'

Mrs Dance, a little wiry woman, got one of the men to lift a sack on to her back and she carried it, $2\frac{1}{4}$ cwt, about seventy-five yards down the road to her cottage.

Swine Fever among pigs was prevalent as the nineteenth century came to an end. In 1892 the Squire heard that the best way to prevent the fever was to cut a little off the end of the pigs' tails and nick a little from their ears. It was still the age of blood-letting in case of disease. Jim Harris was chosen to catch and hold the little pigs while the Squire, with a carving knife, drew the blood. The

Squire didn't believe in half measures and he was cutting great chunks of flesh from the pigs' ears and tails.

'I shouldn't cut quite so much off them, Gaffer, if I was thee,' Jim ventured.

'Shut your mouth, Jim, or I'll serve thee the same,' the Squire replied.

Jim left many years ago now but he never forgot that day at Middle Farm. Someone reported the matter and the Squire was prosecuted for cruelty to animals. The old man – he was an old man now – despite his eccentric ways had pride. His pride was hurt. He would show all and sundry that he wasn't cruel to animals. In Tun Flun (Ten Furlong field) he organized a show. Jim never forgot that either. There had never been a show before in the village. Neighbouring parishes had their flower shows, but this was different. His men penned cattle, sheep, horses, pigs and poultry in the field. Their job was to look after the stock. He ordered them to cut long nut sticks from the wood and act as his stockmen, and he dressed the men in white smocks. Tables were laid in the barn where joints of beef, hams and loaves of bread were all free to the visitors. Jack Fox spent his time with a yoke and two buckets carrying cider from the barn to the field. Trotting races for the farmers' cobs were organized, as well as hurdle races and sack races. The village wheelwright brought his Penny Farthing bike and raced against men from the next village. There was a tug-of-war between the Squire's men and the neighbouring estate men.

Squire Yeomans was the head of a large well-known family. This was his final fling. Shortly afterwards he was out for a ride in the governess cart with the male nurse who looked after him. Along Beckford Way where the open ditch runs down to the brook there is an ancient ash tree; it was here the old Squire breathed his last breath. Just the memory of this eccentric remained for another fifty years, but now those who worked for him are all gone. There is no longer a Squire at Ayshan.

CHAPTER SIX

The War Memorial

The First World War had been over for six years and the villagers were anxious to erect some sort of war memorial. At a meeting in the School Room three sites were suggested. One was on the green by the village Cross, another in a little orchard near the post office, while a third suggestion was on the village pound. As is common on such occasions voices were raised and arguments ensued. The widows and parents of those who had given the supreme sacrifice wanted their way, as is understandable.

'At the Cross near the church where we all go to worship,' was Georgina Coney's suggestion. Her husband was one of the casualties of the war in France.

''Tis a quiet peaceful place in Albert Checketts' orchard anant the Post Office,' old Blenheim Hapgood replied.

George Moseley, the chairman of the meeting, was a landowner and farmer of some substance and had come from the Midlands to a rather grand house. George's garden was adjacent to the old pound, an enclosure where stray animals were impounded in Victorian times. He, being relatively new to the village, thought that the pound belonged to him; it had been annexed by a previous owner of Lammas Hey. His son Frank farmed Home Farm. 'I am quite willing to give to the parish the land known as The Pound for the erection of a war memorial. I think that it would be an ideal site.'

'I would like to second that proposal and thank Mr Moseley for his generous offer,' Tom Arrow commented.

A lot of muttering went on in the schoolroom that evening. Pedlar Price, a left wing activist of the 1920s, rose to speak, 'With respect to you, Mr Moseley, The Pound is not yours to give away, it belongs to the parish.'

Alf Norton added, 'It unt yours to give. Pedlar is quite right and our old man, what 'as bin dead a few years, minded the time when Doctor Richardson's 'oss was put in that thur pen.'

George Moseley replied, 'It's on my deeds, but the question is – do we want to put the memorial there? It's a fine site near the school and it overlooks the Cotswolds.'

A chorus came from Pedlar, Blenheim, and Fred and Jack Chapel. Albert Hedgecock from the pub said, 'No. We want the cross to go on the village green anant the old preaching cross.'

'We will take a vote.' Harold Perry, churchwarden, proposed and it was seconded by Joe Yeomans.

The vote was in favour of The Pound, but Pedlar Price rose to his feet and said, 'I demand a referendum.'

Jasper Hill said in a stage whisper, 'What the hell's a referendum?'

'Shut thee rattle,' Harold Norton said to him among the hubbub of the meeting. 'We be gwain to vote on it.'

The day came when all the folk on the electoral roll were able to say which site they preferred for the war memorial. Site one was the village green; site two was Albert Checketts' orchard; site three was The Pound. The men who were in favour of the memorial being built on the village green met in Albert Hedgecock's thatched pub known as The Wagon and Horses. Jack Fox, the rough carpenter who worked on Manor Farm for Tom Arrow and Harry Castle, was supping from a quart mug of cider – he always started with a quart!

'What dost think of Master Moseley claiming our village Pound. I mustn't say too much about it 'cos our gaffer, Tom Arrow, is pretty thick with him. Mind, Tom Arrow knows different. His father's donkey was impounded when Tom was but a bwoy chap.'

Jack Chapel replied, 'I work for Master Moseley and he's a good gaffer but of course he come here from Brumijum and you can't expect him to know the history of The Pound.'

Pedlar Price was a Londoner by birth, now a fruit grower who ran a Model T Ford for weddings, and took some of the village women shopping at Cheltenham on some Saturdays. He told the men in the pub that he was going to have some posters made and stick them up in the village. The posters would say 'Support the Memorial on the Village Green' and 'The Pound belongs to the Parish'. He also composed some humorous poetry about George Moseley.

Voting day came. The folk in favour of The Pound site had the majority. George Moseley, Tom Arrow, Harold Perry and others formed a committee to raise the money to erect a suitable memorial. It was decided that the memorial with the names of the ones killed in the war should be of Portland Stone. An estimate of £120 was obtained from a local stonemason.

The money was soon raised and the site was cleared. There was one hitch, however; according to Tom Woodcock, the Honourable Treasurer, as Tom called him, had been mixing the sugar with the sand! An unintentional pun when cement, sand and stone were at stake.

Meanwhile, Pedlar Price called a meeting of the men who favoured the village green site for the memorial. Again, they met in The Wagon and Horses: Pedlar, Sapper, Alf Norton, Eli Thatcher, the ladder and hurdle maker, George Meadows ex-Royal Marines, the boot and shoe repairer known as 'the Snob', Jim Beckford and others. It was decided by this little group that in time they would erect a memorial on the green. Pedlar had an idea and went to visit Sapper. Sapper, a master plasterer, was working in the barn making concrete bird-baths. Two great reconstructed stone balls stood on either side of his gateway giving an almost stately feel as one walked up the drive to his cottage. Sapper was a master craftsman who later did the cornice work at Stratford's theatre.

'I've bin thinking, Sapper, do you reckon you could make a war

Cattle and a horse graze in the apple orchard in springtime

Villagers assemble for the unveiling of the war memorial

41

memorial? This is on the Q.T. mind, for God's sake don't let Moseley, Arrow, Castle and that lot know. I want you to do the job undercover. We have got twelve quid between us. You can do it.'

Sapper, the little ex-Royal Engineer, thought a while and replied, 'Oi, I be willing. Thee knowst, Pedlar, that some of the gravestones in the churchyard be my work, the names done beautiful in leadwork. I'll tell thee what, Pedlar, I'll get one done by mid-summer afore the one is built in The Pound.'

Pedlar then started to recite a jingle he had composed on the committee erecting the one on The Pound:

Oh, ain't you gwain to put the granite chippings up?
Oh, when you gwain to put the granite chippings up?

The fact was it was Sapper who was going to use granite chippings.

Behind locked doors the men who had met in The Wagon and Horses worked with Sapper on his war memorial. The most vocal of the workers was George Meadows, the Snob. He had a monthly pension from the Marines; when his pension was paid he spent half of it at The Wagon and Horses. The language of the ex-Royal Marine was so colourful Albert Hedgecock had a swear box in the bar. This box was partly filled on pension nights with pennies from George. Whenever the question of The Pound was mentioned and who owned it, George's swear words were enough to turn the air in the bar blue. Blenheim Hapgood said one night in the pub that he thought The Pound was a damn fool site for the memorial.

'What dos't myun, Blenheim? Thee knowst as well as me that The Pound belongs to the parish and why should we go cap in hand to Master Moseley who an't bin yer long enough to get his seat warm.' These words from Eli Thatcher were the words of a man who, according to Jim Beckford, had been in the village long before the Crimean War.

Sapper worked in his barn with primitive tools. George the

Snob was chosen to mix the reconstituted stone. Sapper's mixing board he called 'his spot'. He used wooden templates to form the shapes of the mixture of granite chippings, cement and sand.

It was finished, as he had promised, by mid-summer. The memorial on a square base below the upright cross had a wreath of laurel leaves cunningly encircling the cross. Tom Woodcock said it was a masterpiece. Sapper, that little man who enjoyed the local cider too much and made wine from his garden crops, his beetroot, parsnips and the damsons off his orchard trees, showed his handiwork to the chosen few.

The village green was a triangular grassy area near the cross and at the entrance to the churchyard. On Whit Saturday the cricket team had an all-day match with Alcester and Ragley Park. This was an annual event, a fixture looked forward to by the villagers. George Moseley, the gentleman from Lammas Hey, gave a splendid salad lunch, real ham, lettuce and the lot. Anyone attending the match was welcome to stay and have lunch. The meal was served by Gwen and Mollie Moseley, George's daughters-in-law, Bunch Yeomans and Barbara Cox.

About 2.30 that afternoon Harold Perry, the Vicar's brother-in-law, was mowing around the graves in the churchyard. He could hear the sound of men working on the village green. A foundation was being made for Sapper's war memorial and Pedlar and George the Snob were mixing concrete.

'What's going on?' Harold called to the men.

'We be putting the foundations in for the War Memorial,' Sapper replied.

'But the vote was for a memorial on The Pound,' Harold answered.

'It's going here. That's our decision and nobody can stop us. This, like The Pound, is parish land,' George the Snob replied angrily.

'Stop at once. I'll fetch the police. You have no right to put a memorial here.'

This outraged the ex-servicemen and George the Snob walked towards Harold and threatened him, saying, 'I was fighting for my country in South Africa before your ass was as big as a sixpence. Don't you tell me what to do you Brumijum Townee.'

The concrete foundations on the green were set hard by the Sunday morning. George Moseley spoke to Harold Perry about the work done by Sapper and Pedlar's gang. 'You were in the churchyard yesterday afternoon, Harold, why didn't you stop the men from what's an illegal act?'

'I couldn't, sir. And besides, George the Snob threatened me and you know what he's like when he's been drinking – they tell me that it was the week for his pension.'

'I do understand that, Harold, but something must be done to stop these hooligans. Tomorrow is Whit Monday and the district surveyors' office will be closed, but I'll put a stop to this. What about the police, Harold, did you inform them?'

'No,' Harold replied, adding, 'It's no good talking to the local constable for he came by on his bike dressed in civvies, it being his day off, and he will be helping George the Snob to get rid of his pension in The Wagon and Horses tonight.'

By the next weekend the village roadman, on instructions from the surveyor, had turfed over the concrete square on the green. Sapper's memorial stood in his yard, partly covered with a Union Jack. Every Sunday he, Pedlar, George the snob and others sat on a couple of pig benches around the memorial drinking home-made wine. That hot summer soon scorched the grass over the concrete square and Walt Chandler said that the evidence of that Saturday afternoon remained, it was a feature. The fact that no memorial was ever built on the green is not quite true, for the scorched square of turf was there as Sapper's token. When he came down the road from The Wagon and Horses smoking his cherry pipe (an enormous pipe which held half an ounce of tobacco) Sapper stood to attention, saluted the village green and sang 'Mademoiselle from Armentieres, Parlez-vous'. It was something that the older villagers will never forget.

The months following saw the unveiling of the memorial at The Pound, an impressive ceremony performed by a local general. The dedication read, 'These men were a wall unto us by night and

day'. The supporters of the village green site who had had
relatives killed during the war refused to have their names put on
the memorial on The Pound. Stubborn you may say, or shall we
record that they had the courage of their convictions.

CHAPTER SEVEN

Jimmy Wasley

Jimmy Wasley had served his country in the First World War, first of all as a trooper in the Yeomanry, where he lived a lot of his life on the back of a horse, a little man in mole-skin trousers and a bushman's hat.

'I got my Commission in the field of battle out in Salonika,' he told Henry Richardson, the doctor's son. Henry knew Jimmy for they rode together following the local fox hounds. 'I'll tell you what happened,' Jimmy said. 'The major in our mob had been master of the foxhounds and I had risen to sergeant. "What are you doing in the ranks, Wasley?" the major asked me.' Jimmy had been a fearless rider over hill and vale, but he had no thought of being an officer. '"I'm commissioning you in the field and from now on you are Lieutenant Wasley," he told me.'

Henry said, 'Your days following the pack over the hill stood you in good stead.'

'You know, Henry, what I think of a good horse and how we looked after our horses compared with the Turks.'

In the 1920s Jimmy Wasley had been bailiff for a retired Army captain who owned an estate and lived at The Hall. If his life working for the captain is described as a 'comfortable job' that's well put. Henry Richardson told his story, as follows:

Jimmy Wasley was more or less his own boss. The captain was quite happy that his bailiff went hunting two days a week with me. I saw what crops Jimmy grew on hill and vale. One crop of wheat was so heavy it was the talk of the district. The stooks were so close together when Jimmy's men took their wagons to the field that before the wagons could go through the gate the men had to pitch the sheaves onto the wagon in the road. I'm telling you that is the truth and, as one of his men said, 'The truth needs no study.'

'Twas muck from his Shorthorn herd that did it, and he folded Oxford Down sheep on turnips and sprout stems. I'll tell another record he held.

Every year, Jimmy won the prize money and the cup for the heaviest crop of mangolds in Britain. Carters' Tested Seeds organized the competition. Fields of mangolds grown on Carters Seeds could be entered. The heaviest crop Jimmy grew was nearer fifty tons per acre than forty. The captain encouraged Jimmy to enter every year and allowed him the prize money, a nice little nest egg.

Jimmy was critical of modern farming methods and of the modern farmer who didn't hang his jacket on the hedge and pitch and load hay all day long like he did. Pershore Fair on 26 June was a Red Letter Day on the calendar. Jimmy bought cart colts from Gloucester, broke them in, worked them until they were five years old and then, if he could spare one, he sold it for the brewers drays and railway drays of Birmingham. One gelding named Smiler he was loathe to part with but he knew that it would command a good price at the fair. Old Ponto, who lived in Jimmy's granary, took Smiler to Pershore Fair. Henry told the story.

I took Jimmy in my pony and trap to the fair. Apart from selling the cart-horse, Jimmy was anxious to pick up a good hunter, not a weight-carrier – Jimmy was only nine stone – but a horse which could take him up the slopes of Bredon Hill and hopefully be at the kill with the hounds. The cart-horse Smiler made a good price going to pull a brewer's dray in Birmingham. I looked around the hunters and nags with Ponto. Ponto declared that he had never seen so many left-handed 'osses in his life. I knew what the old man meant.

As we drove in the pony and trap past the Three Tuns Hotel a horse and dray with cabbages passed us on our way to the vegetable market. 'Stop and follow that dray,' Jimmy said to me. We turned round along Broad Street and caught the horse and dray as the driver was unloading his cabbages.

'You have a good horse there, I reckon,' Jimmy said to the driver, a market gardener.

'Oi, her's a mare I bred meself. Her mother stole the 'oss'. Jimmy knew that it meant that the mare had got to a stallion when she was what was known as 'in use'.

'What stallion was that then? A thoroughbred, I'll gamble.'

'Oi. 'Twas one belonging to the race'oss trainer over the hill.'

Jimmy's mind was working eighteen-to-the-dozen knowing that the stallion was none other than his father-in-law's. 'You want to sell the mare? I'll give you a good price. Take her out of the shafts and run her up the road.'

Jimmy gave me the wink and said quietly, 'I'll buy her. It's what I want.'

'How much?' Jimmy asked the owner.

'Well they tells me in the village that her's worth over forty quid.'

'I'll give you fifty,' Jimmy replied.

'If I sell her what about my dray?'

'My man Ponto will go home with you and ride the mare to my place.' Jimmy held out his hand, the market gardener clasped it as Jimmy called out 'Sold'.

The following week Jimmy and Henry rode their hunters to the top of Bredon Hill. The mare proved a stayer. Jimmy entered his

Members of the hunt ford a stream on their shining horses

new steed at the local hunt's point-to-point. After winning at that event he won the adjacent hunt point-to-point. Henry records how he persuaded Jimmy to have a go at the amateur riders' race at Cheltenham races. The local paper announced his win, 'Farmer Wins Coveted Prize with a Mare From a Market Gardener's Dray'.

It is often said that farmers make bad gardeners. This didn't apply to Jimmy Wasley according to Henry: 'Did you ever see dahlias like those grown by the bailiff from The Hall? Jimmy had a secret which few people knew. The recognized dahlia growers never knew that his recipe for growing dahlias was simple. Jimmy had a hogshead barrel in his garden filled with rain water. In the barrel he put soot and sheep beltings – the soiled wool from the backside of his ewes – to make a liquid manure. At the flower show Jimmy swept the deck with his flowers and ventured further afield to Shrewsbury Show.'

This little man, with tall Henry by his side, became somewhat of a legend in the vale villages.

CHAPTER EIGHT

Blenheim and Laughing Tom

Tom Yeomans, affectionately known as Laughing Tom, farmed about twenty acres of land at the foot of the hill, including eight acres of orchard. He was related to Henry Richardson, both being descendants of the Squire.

Blenheim Hapgood, whose family had lived in the little thatched cottage near Tom's holding at The Glen for many years, propelled his arthritic body along the land with the aid of an ash plant. He was driving Laughing Tom's herd of shorthorns.

Henry Richardson, who never did much work except following Jimmy Wasley over the hill on his nag when the hunt met at The Wagon and Horses, spent a part of his misspent youth in Laughing Tom's Cider House, and he described it to me:

It's a tumbledown thatched cottage where Blenheim and Laughing Tom stored the hogshead barrels of cider. A press stood in what was the kitchen and outside the cider mill crushed the apples. Laughing Tom's nag, an iron-grey gelding called

51

Sport, pushed rather then pulled the stone around the stone trough crushing the cider apples from the orchard at The Glen. Blenheim scooped the pomace he called 'pommy' with a wooden shovel and used a wooden bucket to take it to the press. Here he made what they called cheeses of pulp in layers between oat straw ready for the huge press to squeeze the juice from the pulp.

'A few pints of this, Henry, when it's been made a while ull make thee talk about thee Grandfather, and I be one as knowed him.'

Blenheim never minced his words for when Jack Chapel came to the Cider House to see Laughing Tom about a four-gallon barrel of cider he made a sarcastic remark to Blenheim. It was a time when a second world war looked to be probable. Some men, Reservists, had been called up. Jack, looking at Blenheim, said, 'Hast got thee papers yet, Blenheim?'

Blenheim, never short of an answer, replied, 'What papers? Who was it had rheumatic and belly-ache in the last war and got Doctor Richardson to get thee out of the Army and then never voted for him at the council election, and besides what bist a doing with that graft? Thee bist a rabbit ass, Jack, to be sure.'

At Christmas time, Henry Richardson spent hours in Laughing Tom's Cider House. It was here the farm men congregated after the stock had been fed on Christmas Day. Here Henry listened to the wisdom of the ancients: tales of Blenheim's father, Aaron, who shepherded Cotswold ewes on the hill; wet winters when they carried the sheep off the turnip field on hurdles because of the wet; tales of Shadow the fiddler, who played in the village orchestra in the gallery of the church before the harmonium came; village families who reared the children in one up, one down cottages, and one family who shared a herring for Sunday dinner. Henry had a certain breeding and considered himself a historian because his family had lived in the village for five hundred years.

One Christmas afternoon, the men were sitting on pig benches and corn sacks in the Cider House. Henry and Laughing Tom were

The postman manages to include himself in this picture of men tiling the malthouse

Crowds gather at a cattle market in the 1920s

dozing. Blenheim went to milk the red shorthorn cows and came back to the Cider House saying, 'Gaffer, Old Ada, one of they cows, is on a bulling. We shall have to take her to Harry Castle's bull at the Manor.

Henry shook himself, stood up and said, 'We can't take a cow to the bull on Christmas Day!'

'Don't thee talk so daft, Henry. Thee talks like the Foolish Women. Her ull be gone off in the morning. Now you chaps give us a hand down the road. We shall have to let Ada have her annual yard a bull.'

Laughing Tom replied, 'Well, it ull be best to catch her this time round.' Turning to Henry, he said, 'Can you give us a hand?'

Henry recalled the pantomime of he and Blenheim and Laughing Tom driving Ada and another cow to the Hereford bull at Manor Farm. As the unsteady men passed Tom Woodcock's cottage he came to the gate.

'Where dost think you chaps be gwain?' he asked.

'Just the mon we wanted,' Blenheim replied. 'Thee come with us and loose Harry Castle's bull into the yard. We got a cow on a bulling.'

Tom followed the little group down the road and released the bull who was not too inclined to serve the cow.

'He knows it's Christmas Day,' Henry joked.

'Don't thee talk so foolish. Nobody ud think that thy father was a doctor,' Blenheim replied.

The two cows circled the yard, riding each other round. The bull didn't seem interested. Just then the Tewkesbury Tabor and Tut band started playing 'Oh Come All Ye Faithful' in the drive outside Harry Castle's house.

'Thurs a caper, unt it Tom?' Blenheim said to Harry's stockman.

'Perhaps it will give an urge to the bull, the music,' were Henry's words.

Laughing Tom said, 'I'll tell ya what it is, chaps like Henry be born and they got to be kept.'

At that moment, as the band played 'Come let us adore him' the bull mounted and served Ada.

'That's it then,' Tom Woodcock said.

'No, let him have another go. One for luck. One swallow don't make a summer.'

'That's true, Blenheim. Now the bull's in the humour. Damn it, the tups on the hill serves the ewes all night.'

'That's as may be,' the stockman said to Laughing Tom, 'but I want to get back to my tea.'

The bull obliged and the party, sobering up, took the cows home.

The following year Tom Yeomans' orchard was laden with apples, pears and plums. He sent his produce to the Smithfield Market all graded and well packed. He and Blenheim sorted the apples, the small ones went with the genuine cider varieties for cider. Henry Richardson fetched the market money every Saturday and took it to Laughing Tom at The Glen. He tells the story that for several weeks the auctioneer told him to tell Tom to pick the fruit under-ripe because it had to travel to the towns up north by train. He delivered the message once more, but Laughing Tom replied, 'I beunt a gwain to pick my pears until they be mella, they beunt worth a hat full of crabs. Thee tell that auctioneer fella that I bin at this game too long not to know when to pick pears.'

Every piece of fruit went from The Glen fit for the table. Laughing Tom never altered, thinking it murder to pick fruit a little under-ripe.

CHAPTER NINE

George Fox who became a Champion

George was born in Pear Tree Cottage, where the village street climbs up Bredon Hill. 'I was born in 1898, the third son of Charles, always called the miracle baby by Doctor Richardson who delivered me – I was a bit premature and underweight, the doctor thought I was a goner. He apparently smacked my ass and I cried. That was eighty-seven years ago.

'At the village school I suppose I did like the rest of the pupils, soon learnt to read and write and reckon up. Mind you, after tea in the spring and summer Dad had us bwoys on the allotment until dark, planting, weeding, pulling, cutting. The allotment, known as Hammer and Length, was where we grew strawberries and asparagus for market. We have done some work down there. Dad wheeled his produce up the road on a wheelbarrow. Spring onions for Mother to tie, etc. One day he wanted to leave the barrow on the land, so he took his bike down from home on the barrow in order to ride home at night.'

'Now, you know the blacksmith in the next village. Well, Tom had an arrangement with the local paper, *The Standard*, to report anything that happened funny like. The paper had a column "Notes by the Chiel". So Dad was in "the Chiel" that week. I've often told ya, mind what you be at Fred, you'll be in the Chiel.

'Of course we went to chapel, but that wasn't lively enough for Dad so he joined the Salvation Army. Of course, as a boy I didn't often go to town, so I went to chapel Sunday School, but Dad's stories about the early days in the Salvation Army I remember. The local corps had an officer who had been a prize-fighter. The band came over from the town to our village. The officer had a nickname, Toad Pelt. At Blacksmiths Lane the little ring had played a hymn and Toad Pelt was praying. You remember Cocky who lived at the bottom of the village? Well, he and some of the other hobbledehoys walked backwards and forwards through the ring of worshippers. Toad Pelt hit Cocky smack on the nose, then finished his prayer, saying, "In the Word it says 'The churning of milk bringeth forth butter, the wringing of the nose bringeth forth blood'." Cocky's nose did bleed!

'Thur was some trouble, mind, in the early days but they put some stunts on to win the people over. Thee Dad, Fred, he was dressed as a policeman one time in Assum (Evesham). He marched in front of the band with Tom of the Fens, a converted criminal, handcuffed to him. I can see it now. Tom of the Fens in prison clothes, broad arrows and the lot. Stirring times!'

George was silent for a moment and then said, 'I left school in 1911 when I was but thirteen. I worked with the 'osses along of Walt Chandler plough-driving that winter, then the gaffer, my Uncle Tom, put me with the men sprout-picking on Bredon Hill. 1911 was a hot, dry summer and vegetables were short in the winter. Tis allus damp where there are stones and it was like that in fifteen acres behind Grafton Firs. Mind, there's not a lot of mould, but Walt and me we ridged the ground with a bouting out plough and the men planted the sprout plants on the ridges. That was my first experience of sprout picking.' He paused, then said, 'I suppose I'm still the champion, I've got the Silver Cup.

'On the dark winter mornings it was my job to fetch the 'osses

The blacksmith was traditionally the collector of all the village gossip

in for bait. They were in Didcot Ham anant the brook. I'll admit I've allus bin afraid of the dark. As a bwoy twas unkid in our old cottage groping about with a candle, then pulling my boots over the chilblains and going down Gipsies Lane to fetch the 'osses. I used to give young Spud who lived with us a penny to go to Didcot Ham with me. You see on the wet meadows I didn't like the sight of the bobbety lanterns – some calls um will-o'-the-wisps. Then Uncle Jack Fox used to tell tales of spring-heeled Jack in Gipsies Lane. Mind, Uncle Jack was different to Dad and me who never drank. He was often as drunk as a Bob Howler. When young Arthur Harris left school he drove plough for Walt and I was given charge of a scratch team of 'osses. It was only likely that Walt ploughed with the four best in the stable.'

It was now that what I'd suspected about George became so real. Here was Dogberry straight out of *Much Ado About Nothing*; George was still using the language of Shakespeare. It is true that the only time George had been to Stratford was to the Mop, but the way of the bard rested a little on his shoulders. He spoke of his team, the Foremost, the Lash horse, the Body horse and the Filler. The Shakespearean words flowed from George, as he used words like 'anant' for next to, 'moot' for sticking clay; 'yaffle' or 'stock eagle' for the woodpecker.

George described his team of horses. 'To say they were the occud squad, that's putting it mild, and my plough boy was old, Ponto, a man of sixty who was what was known as a mental deficient. He did put it on, but it seems that he was crossed in love as a young man. Ponto did boys' jobs about the farms, taking the 'osses to the blacksmith, fetching the milking cows from the field and plough-driving. Some days he'd be all right and another he'd be as occud as a tup. One day ploughing on the hill, Ponto left his matches on the wall and the sun set them on fire. "It's the Russians," he said, and we did no more work that day. Our team of horses had Dick, a gelding with a big knee, as foremost, then came little Blackbird, who had one eye, as lash horse, the body horse was Tom the Nag, a light-legged dray horse, and old Captain was filler at the back. Captain was strong, he had a ridged back, and a ride down the hill on that was painful. When you are ploughing with four horses the work is done in "beds", casting and ridging. Walt and Arthur started and finished the beds or stetches for me. Our scratch team was all right when the work was straightforward.

'When the war started in 1914 the Army took two of Walt's best young horses for France and the gaffer had to buy a couple of old 'uns at Gloucester. A mare named Violet kicked flashes but me and Walt tamed her. My two brothers were called up. Charles was killed soon after landing in the Dardanelles and Tom went to France. When I went for a medical I thought that I'd be in khaki. I've allus suffered with me feet, got 'ammer toes, and old Doctor Richardson who brought me into the world was on the medical tribunal. When I stripped in front of the board the old Doctor said, "Send him back to the land, he will be a nuisance in the Army with feet like that." Another doctor asked me how I managed to walk all day behind the plough. I thought a bit and said, "I hangs on to the implement, Sir." Old Doctor Richardson got a good many chaps out of the Army, one in particular who was supposed to have rheumatics, but that cleared up after the Armistice.

'When the war was over my girlfriend and me got married in the village church. We were the last couple the old parson married before he died. After a time we rented a council house at ten bob a week and I was only getting thirty bob. It was too dear and many's the time we went to bed hungry. So it was back to the little cottage, two-up two-down, an earth floor in the kitchen, but it was only three bob a week. I carried the water from the pump in the road and we shared the bucket privy with a cantankerous 'ooman next door.

'My missus worked hard – what was known as charring, and grew plants in the garden for sale. Our simple life was happy, with fellowship at the village chapel. The gaffers went in for market gardening, growing sprouts, peas, strawberries, wallflowers, beans and cabbages. While the other men worked in a gang, a lot of my time was spent drilling, planting, horse-hoeing with young Fred leading the horse. We covered some ground.

Early mornings in June and July we were strawberry-picking at four o'clock. I've been in Assum market on a Monday with a load of fresh-picked fruit at half-past six. We never worked on a Sunday. You see I suppose I've always bin an early riser and it was my job during the strawberry season to waken Uncle Tom for him to take the fruit to Cheltenhem Market.'

'But George, didn't you go with a horse and dray to market?'

'That was Assum, but Uncle Tom took the fruit in his Sunbeam car to Cheltenham in 1924.'

George told how when the new council houses were built he had cne. 'That was an improvement for the family 'cos we had the 'lectric. We put a shilling in the meter for light and that lasted a week if there were 25-watt bulbs in the rooms. Mind you, we had no sanitation, a bucket lavatory at the back and very little garden to empty the bucket, and we fetched the water from a standpipe.

'I was allus first up at the council houses and very often the tap was froze at the standpipe. I used to thaw the tap with a match and newspaper. All eyes ud be on me and you can guess the rest. The other tenants then came with their buckets to get water, but it was allus me who thawed the tap.

'In those days we picked sprouts piece work, sixpence a pot of forty pounds. That was before we had the twenty pound net. I could pick thirty pots a day and earn fifteen shillings, which was much better than the five bob a day on day work.

'There was not a lot to do bar work except football on Saturdays and chapel on Sundays. I had a good wife and family. Oh, one thing I enjoyed was a Woodbine; I used to light up every pot a sprouts I picked, that would be fourpence for ten, thirty a day. I suppose that was a shilling gone up in smoke out of fifteen and I soon gave that up. After tea in winter my job was to go and take the rabbits from the wire snares on the hill. Master Castle set the snares in the day with Uncle Jack. I had one shilling and sixpence a night for rabbiting. We used a carbide bicycle lamp to go round the wires. Young Fred used to come along.

'Our land got what we call "sprout-sick" after years of cropping. The gaffer planted some at a village called Great Washbourne. The

Eva Lawrence and Will Smith smile for the camera on their wedding day

Best bonnets, caps and Union Jacks were the order of the day on the Band of Hope's annual outing

farmer there kept sheep which he hurdled on roots. The ground was kind, the sheep were like donkeys. We had a master crop of Brussels. On one January day I picked forty pots or eighty nets of sprouts by dark. Uncle Tom told the story to the growers and merchants in Assum Market. The report in the Assum *Journal* resulted in letters to say it couldn't be done. Jack Hodges, a grower and merchant, decided to form a committee and organise a sprout-picking competition to find the champion sprout-picker. The field of sprouts chosen was at Haselor near Cropthorne, the day was cold after frost. There were about twenty competitors, including two women. The BBC recorded the event and the filming was done for a newsreel. Robin Whitworth was the commentator, Jack Hodges was the M.C. and in his humorous way made the scene. When the whistle went we all started picking. I was the only one in shirt sleeves. We picked for two hours and then the stewards weighed the nets. Mr Harry from the Bon Marche was a committee man. Here was a man who was such a friend to the workers of the vale, providing warm clothes at low prices. I remember Jack shouting through the mike: "Enter unto the field of battle Mr Harry from the Bon Marche. His trousers are still coming down." Mr Harry had the last laugh and he was a business man, he gave me a new overcoat when I won the competition. In the Assum *Journal* Mr Harry stated "The Sprout Picking Champion was wearing a Bon Marche overcoat." Course I didn't wear it to work but it was good for Sundays. When I was announced the winner and spoke on the BBC the film of the championship was shown at the Regal cinema. I had my leg pulled and was called a film star. Beachcomber in the *Daily Express* took the mickey, but it was all good fun. I did disappoint some at the dinner when I was presented with the Silver Cup as I wouldn't drink wine from it. Well, I never did drink; I had signed the pledge when I was sixteen.'

CHAPTER TEN

Phil Richardson the Solitary

Phil Richardson, the younger son of Doctor Richardson and a direct descendant of the Squire on his mother's side, stood out as a gentleman of the old school. Yet Phil never achieved his aim to work in the Colonial Office.

'I attended the village school,' he told me, 'then had private tuition and did very well in languages, especially French. Of course I was disappointed not getting a post in the Civil Services overseas. Father being a widower could do little for me, he had to bring up the family. It meant that I drifted into working the small farms. My brother Henry looked after a dairy and delivered milk. I worked in the orchards, reared turkeys and grew crops on the arable. It wasn't my scene, I was in love.'

'In love, Phil, with whom? Not the thatcher's daughter.'

'No. You know me, I was in love with Bredon Hill. Housman was only partly right when he wrote "Summer Time on Bredon". Bredon is magic all the year round. Every minute I could get after work on the farm, Bredon Hill became my classroom. There is a little outcrop of stone below the beech trees. The circle of trees known as The Cuckoo Pen stands above that outcrop as a guardian angel. The outcrop has been my seat for years, more years than I can remember. It was here I read the works of Plato, Homer and all the old masters. I contemplated the world after the First World War, spent time meditating on God. Summer nights after halcyon days when to sleep in my bed seemed to be wasting my life. The sun came up over the Cotswolds and I rose from that short thyme-scented turf after sleeping neath the stars. Town folk miss so much with their artificial existence.'

He stood there in his orchard, a man in his early eighties with a back as straight as steel, a clipped beard, a hacking jacket and a pair of Lovat trousers. 'The village I knew as a boy had a stream down the road and little causeways, like Bourton-on-the-Water, to the cottages. Father's ducks swam in the stream and Club Day on Trinity Monday was a Red Letter Day. Father was in the Chair at the dinner of the Conservative Friendly Society. Horse-drawn carriages came from Cheltenham with some of the dignitaries. To see those horses raring to go outside the Plough and Harrow was something. Dad being the village doctor did a lot for nothing for the poor.

'Of course, the accidents in the village were quite minor things, like Mrs Georgina Coney had the chamber-pot collapse under her one night. Prudence, her daughter, fetched Dad who stitched up her bottom. Georgina was known as 'the Merry Widow'. I'd been out hunting that day and remember Father returning from her cottage by the Midland Railway line at four o'clock in the morning!

'After a few years as a member of the hunt, times were bad on the land, my turkeys died of a disease, and I really couldn't afford the luxury of the chase. Mind you, I didn't like to be there at the kill, I enjoyed the ride over the hill and vale. As an old man I'm against blood sports.'

Phil smiled, he was back in his younger days, the young blood of Bredon Hill.

A child stands in the middle of a quiet road which passes through the village

'You never married, Phil,' I prompted.

'No. I was just thinking of some of the young ladies who followed the hounds. There was one who came from the other side of the hill. We kept together, she had a grey mare, three-quarters bred from a thoroughbred. Many's the time we tied our horses up at Fiddlers Nap and spent the morning in that delightful, violet and primrose coppice. It was the last meet of the season at Easter and the floor of the coppice was carpeted with bloom and as we rode back in the evening the sainfoin was just coming into flower on Great Hill. We were going to marry that year, but she contracted T.B., what Father called Consumption, and died the next winter. I walk over the hill and put flowers on her grave when I can. Here am I, a solitary man, living in this big house with my memories.'

A few weeks after this Phil went in to hospital. Here was a man who didn't trust the modern medics, a man with simple needs. The doctor prescribed two pills every night. Phil was dubious of the care in this modern place, especially when the doctor came at night in his shirt sleeves. 'Not like Father,' he said, harking back to the days before the First World War, 'shirt sleeves and braces!' He discharged himself and died alone at home. A solitary life, a solitary death.

CHAPTER ELEVEN

Jim Beckford

CHAPEL ELDER, MUSICIAN, WATER DIVINER

Jim Beckford was born in 1860, left school at eleven, and worked on the land ploughing and driving. He was a most versatile man who in later life was an expert rose grower, grafter of fruit trees, bee-keeper, hedge-layer, local preacher, Sunday School teacher, and gentleman's gardener.

'Working for the Squire as a boy we were supposed to go to church on Sunday. The Parson was so fond of the drink that Sunday School didn't often last for long. Stories are many about Revd Joseph: how he was half-way through the funeral service when he was conducting a wedding and said he was so sorry, he was moved by the Spirit. But fair play, he was good to the poor of the Parish.

'At that time the Methodist church were holding meetings in Attwood's barn. I used to go along and there was a need they said for a chapel to be built in the village. Mind you, Father had been a member of the village orchestra that played on the balcony of the church. He played the fiddle, and later on I played the big bass viol. At that time a missionary came into the parish and he had a tent and needed somewhere to pitch it to hold the meetings. Doctor Richardson had a little orchard anant the road opposite Home Farm where Jack Yeomans' father Bill lived. You know, Bill was a descendant of the Squires of the village, autocratic, a hard man, supposed to be a guardian of the poor. Doctor Richardson and Bill Yeomans were cousins by marriage and that was all, they hated each other. The Doctor gave Master Hobbs, the missionary, permission to put his tent in his orchard. 'But,' everyone said, 'The doctor has no time for dissenters, chapel folk. He must be gone off his head.' But Doctor Richardson's head was all right: his scheme was that the singing of chapel hymns and the noise from the meetings would aggravate Bill Yeomans. Bill Yeomans was a High Church man and couldn't abide the chapel folk. As a young man, I remember the singing of hymns and the harmonium and my fiddle-playing swept across the road to Bill Yeomans and he was helpless to stop it. Some nights we were there till the pubs closed and there were about eight or ten converts to the Faith, including me.

'I was a bit over twenty when Hobbs came to the tent in the doctor's orchard. We had no chapel and Master Yeomans and Parson Joseph were aginst us. We built a little Chapel in an orchard belonging to a farmer and I became a local preacher. Looking back, I remember most of the chapel folk lived by the Cross at the bottom of the village while the church people lived at the top of the parish. Just picture a Sunday in winter: we walked up the causeway by the stream carrying our candle lanterns meeting the Church folk as they came from the top. There was a rift and sometimes our cause was under attack. One of our members was hit by a stone thrown through the window by Yeomans' groom.

'We were unlearned men and women who experienced conversion, perhaps too eager to alter the world; at meetings in the open air statements were made which should not have been. One man died and one of the speakers in the open air declared that he was gone to Hell. This made Revd Joseph, the Parson, furious. Revd

John followed Joseph and he refused to bury chapel folk who had not been baptised. We've come a long way from then, thank God.

'I was employed then on Manor Farm in charge of the men and shepherd of a flock of Cotswold sheep. Bredon was where I worked, where I thought and it was a kind of little kingdom which was my own because I was alone with nature, the sheep, the peewits, the larks and the changing clouds and weather. Yes, I drove the bullocks at plough there when I was a small boy and was often glad to eat a swede from the sheep-folds. The Cotswold tegs when they were fat stood above their hurdles like donkeys. When I saw the bees on the great boar thistles on the hill it made me think that to produce honey in my garden among the fruit trees would be interesting. You know those boar thistles on Bredon are said to be special, I've heard of carters tying their horses to them. I had been shown by my Dad how to make a straw skep, or beehive, and had made and sold a few. It was late June when young Arthur Harris came one tea time and told me he had seen a swarm of bees settled on a thistle on Spring Hill. Together we went and secured them in a skep and that started my bee-keeping.'

Later Jim Beckford became a gardener and exhibitor of roses. In 1911 Arrow and Castle rented The Manor and he went as gardener to George Moseley, a gentleman who came from the Black Country, who lived at Lammas Hey.

'We grew exhibition roses on that clay and won so many prizes and cups. Our stock came from the hedges, the hip briars growing for free. I budded them and planted them.'

He smiled because everyone likes things for free, and I said, 'I've heard about you and the Dorothy Perkins.'

'Yes. I was in love with that rose; in fact I still am. Mr Moseley had a second-rate orchard at the back of Lammas Hey, he asked my advice. We got trees from Kings Acre Nurseries at Hereford and planted them in place of some that were worn out and I grafted some stocks in the nursery in Moseley's garden with some of the finest varieties.'

'Did you graft that pear tree at the top of Blacksmiths Lane with four varieties?'

He smiled and replied, 'Yes. William, Windsor, Jargenelle and Burgundy.'

There was never a man in the village who had so many strings to his bow as Jim Beckford. I knew some of his achievements. 'Is it true you can graft pears onto hawthorn trees?'

'Of course,' he replied. 'You have heard me tell that when you were in my class at Sunday School. In the orchard next to Harry Castle's house there are four Potmaston Duchess pear trees, I grafted them on hawthorn many years ago.'

I knew that Jim Beckford was most at home when he was at chapel. He who had been a shepherd spoke of 'the Good Shepherd' at Sunday School and what he called his 'topic' was not far removed from the village and fields of his birth. Music was also important.

'Dad played the fiddle on Club Days at Christmas and often at the pub. Sadly he hung his fiddle up at the door when he came home at night but still there was very little comfort in the cottage on winter evenings with five children at home. I suppose had it not been for Mr Hobbs coming and turning us right about face I'd have been like Father.

'Oh, yes, Dad did go to Church and played the big bass viol in the village orchestra up in the gallery of the church. I took up the bass viol when the orchestra was abandoned and the organ was installed in the church. Playing the bass with my two sons on violas and daughter on the 'cello was something that satisfied me no end those Sundays at chapel. So we had an orchestra for social evenings.'

'I remember the little Welsh-like chapel and I remember you saying when bits of plaster fell from the roof "I'm afraid we shall soon have it down on top of us" and you and others worked hard to get the money for a new buildng. Wasn't it to be built where Jim Harris lived?'

'Oh, there was a bit of trouble over that. You see, Harry Castle bought Jim's cottage for a hundred pounds, and Harry was going to have the cottage demolished and the chapel built there. You know, that's anant Lammas Hey where George Moseley lives, in

The fiddler

A healthy-looking flock of sheep follow their shepherd

fact just across his orchard. My gaffer, Master Moseley, being a good churchman didn't really want a chapel next to his orchard and garden. Plans were passed and the chapel was about to be built, but then Master Moseley produced his trump card! He went to see Harry Castle and the chapel committee. I remember it well because I was on that committee. We sat there that night in the chapel, which was falling down, and listened to him. He was an educated man and a good Christian. "Look here, Harry," he said, "You have a good site right here for your new church. Build it after you have knocked this place down."

'"But it's going to cost more money clearing the site and building here!" the committee told him.

'George Moseley was a clever man and he then put forward his plan. "I'll give £100 towards the chapel if it's built here and I'll send a couple of my men to clear the site." Harry Castle and the committee were delighted with his offer which was accepted. Mind you, it didn't please everybody, for Jim Harris's cottage would have been more central for the villagers.

'About that time there was also a bit o' trouble at the church over the proposed building of a lych-gate. Revd Butcher hadn't been here long and a retired farmer from away offered to put a lych-gate by the Cross on the path to the church in memory of his wife. Well, I knew the farmer, a hard man who offered some of his chaps some allotment ground if they voted for him at the district council election. We worked hard that summer pulling up the gorse bushes on the hill and levelling the anthills and then we ploughed it. He lost the election and Doctor Richardson was elected and the next year after we had cleaned the ground he took it off us.

'The path to the church is bounded on both sides by garden land which belonged to Squire Yeomans and now belongs to Arrow and Castle. Some of these townees like Parson Butcher haven't got much up top. When you are dealing with folk born and bred in the place you have to hold the candle to them. There's a right of way to the church and the church property starts at the yew tree. The Parson, when he met a funeral, always came up to the yew tree; Revd Butcher came as far as the road on the footpath right of way. I remember Tom Arrow's father planting the drooping ash trees alongside the footpath when the Squire was at the Manor. Revd Butcher, when he came here from Brumijum, first of all found out that Arrow and Castle were responsible for a tythe payable to him on some land by the brook known as Didcot Ham. The tythe was nine shillings and five pence and that Parson never failed to collect it on 1 January. He said it kept him in postage stamps.

'When the offer was made for the village to have a lych-gate, the Parson informed Arrow and Castle but said if they objected the gate would still be erected. The problem came when Harold Perry, the churchwarden, locked the gate on a right of way. There was a kissing gate beside the double gates, but folks with prams or wheelbarrows going to the cottages on the hill could not manoeuvre through them.

'Harold Perry was brother-in-law to the Parson and came from Brumijum. I suppose he was living on a pension. He kept the churchyard tidy at his own expense but kept rubbing away with his spade at the footpath until Bunch Yeomans, who lived near there, told him that there was room for a wagon and horses to drive up the path, it was as wide as the lane.

'There used to be some laughs concerning Bunch and Harold. I do think he fancied her, but he didn't play his cards right. When he was always borrowing her broom to sweep the path, she told him that soon there would be no bristles in it. Oh, they used to argue, but Bunch had the last laugh. Bunch had a stone statue of a lady in her garden just over the hedge from the churchyard. Harold was coming down the path and looked over the hedge. It was getting twilight and, thinking it was Bunch, he raised his trilby hat as usual and said good-night to the statue. Bunch was gardening a few yards away and split her sides laughing. Harold puffed at his pipe and, dressed as usual in his pepper-and-salt suit and carrying his spade, went on his way to tea with his brother-in-law and spinster sister.

'Alice Chandler who lived on the Hill at Holcombe Nap was

Walt Chandler's wife and their son's wife had recently had a baby. She lived next door. Their only way to Holcombe Nap was the path through the churchyard and the gate was locked. Bunch let the folk from Holcombe Nap come through her garden but a deputation from Holcombe Nap asked the parish council to do something. The council told Harold Perry to unlock the gate. He refused, saying it was locked to prevent stray cattle from coming into the churchyard. The problem was reported to the county council, which resulted in Alderman Brown meeting the parish council, Harold Perry and the Parson. Brown didn't mince his words but told Harold and the Parson that residents from Holcombe Nap would be entitled to smash the gate with an axe to maintain the right of way. The gate remained locked until Harold died.'

Jim Beckford was also known as a water diviner. He sometimes used a V-shaped hazel twig but often his divining apparatus was copper wire around his arm and the top of an umbrella suspended on a silken thread. This we called his dangler and it rotated violently over water.

'When the twig acts', he said, 'it draws all your muscles tight and a strong underground watercourse can bring you to your knees. I don't understand why but know there is so much electricity in my body I can't carry a watch, it just doesn't go. If you hold the twig like a catapult stick by the two ends, hold it tight, the power of the water will spin the twig. I've found water all over the Midlands, and buried treasure. It's a gift I suppose. There are so many things we can't explain. We trust the One above.'

CHAPTER TWELVE

Jarvie Ricketts

GAMEKEEPER AND PIG-KILLER

Jarvie Ricketts had lived at Cobblers Quar, a promontory which stuck out of Bredon Hill facing the Cotswold Edge, as long as I could remember. It seemed to me that he had always been there, and there he would remain. In fact he stayed until approaching one hundred years, then slipped away. His last few months were spent in bed and it was then I visited him. A porcelain pig stood on the bedside table to remind him of the pigs he had dealt with.

'You know,' he said, 'I believe in incarnation and I'd like to come back as a tup (a ram) and be turned out with forty ewes.'

But Jarvie was a romantic with his china-blue eyes and soft voice. Gamekeepers tend to keep their voices down. He was a kind man and maybe that's how he did have his wicked way with the ladies, in the fox-covers of Bredon and, as he told me, among the asparagus bowers of the Vale of Evesham. He never married.

Here in his cottage was a kind of museum of bird traps, spring guns, rabbit nets and his ferrets. He kept a few pigs in a paddock at the back of his cottage. The afternoons I spent with Jarvie in his kitchen are memorable. One afternoon after we had raked over past days on the hill he said, 'It's been like a summer's day talking to you.' I felt the same way; his stories were so vivid.

'Tell me,' I said, 'about the lady with the wig.'

He started his story. 'I was living at Cobblers Quar. It was about eleven o'clock at night. My sister was alive then. We had been in bed about an hour when she called from her bedroom that she had heard a woman calling from the hill. I got up, slipped my trousers on, put on an overcoat and lit the hurricane lantern. In the field at the back of the cottage a woman was calling "I'm lost. I'm lost." "Where are you?" I answered. "By the stream," she replied. It was a moonlight night in November with a touch of frost. The woman came towards me. To be honest, what I saw that night frightened me almost to death. I stood there in front of the woman, frozen-like. Lifting up my hurricane lantern there was the bald-headed woman in the moonlight staring at me. When I got my breath I said, "What are you doing here?" she replied, "I have lost my wig. It's in the water." Following the stream down the hill, I found the wig floating in a water tank. She had been in this tank, there was not a dry stitch on her. I said, "Here's your wig, but where are you steering for?" She replied, "I want to get to Grafton."

'Well, I told her to steer for the stone stile between the elms, which showed up under the moon. "I know the stone stile," she replied and off she went. She was as drunk as a Bob Howler but steady on her feet. I went back to bed but never slept. What made that night so spookey for me was that only the winter before the legendary woman at Benedict's Pool had appeared to me at the full moon.

'The hermit of the hill had warned me about Benedict's Pool in the middle of a coppice. "Never go by there at the full moon," he had said. Well, I'd got my rabbit snares in a field next to the pool and had to collect the rabbits that night. I took the footpath just as the monastery clock struck midnight. I was walking away from the pool carrying a bag of rabbits, when I saw a lady in a white dress approach from the Firs towards Benedict's Pool. I stepped aside from the footpath allowing her to pass and said, "Good evening." She passed a yard away and when I looked back she was gone. Where did she go? When I got home I had to use two hands to get my hat off and I couldn't put it back on for a fortnight. Before I saw the lady my hair was as black as jet, look at it now – white as snow.'

Jarvie was well known in the villages under the hill as a pig-killer. In this capacity he was a professional. He was full of stories of his slaughtering days, like this one.

'Henry Richardson had a boar pig in a pen by the village street. At that time I was busy killing pigs for cottagers. when I passed the pen, it's a funny thing, whether that pig knew what I was up to, but he roared at me like a lion. He was a Gloucester Old Spot several years old. Henry said he could not get anyone to kill him. I said, "I'll kill him if someone will give me a hand." Tom Woodcock came along and I had got a ·303 rifle. I told Tom to get an apple and tempt the boar to the gate. He did that and then I rubbed the apple core on my rope and dangled the rope over the gate. The boar bit at the rope as it was over his snout and I got him tied to the gate. I shot from the ·303 and he was dead and when I cut him up the bullet had gone right up his back bone. Oh, I've been pulled around by pigs but never afraid. It's use you see, it's now or never. The boar was over twenty score pounds, only good for sausages.

'Of course I was used to firing a rifle, it came in handy when we wanted some venison for the bell ringers' supper! The fawns were dropped in the bracken in the park in the spring and I would castrate some of them. We called them avions. Some weeks before the supper I was asked to shoot an avion with my ·303 and with telescopic sights that was no problem. And then there were the rabbits on the hill, which we used to catch with a long net.

'It was like this. Me brother came and said let's go and use the net on the hill. My net was one hundred yards long but this particular night didn't appear to be the right weather for netting. There was quite a moon showing over the Firs but a bit o' breeze. I said that the rabbits would be up on the bank above the big earth

Bacon-curing in the farmhouse kitchen

The club day procession assembles on Whit Thursday

on what was called the Nap. We put the net down and I left me brother in charge, taking my two spaniels around the Nap to drive the rabbits towards the net. When I got three-quarters of the way down the hill the net was gone. I found the net some distance away. Me brother said, "Never seen anything like it! The rabbits came down like a flock of sheep and took the net with them." There were sixty-one rabbits in the net, the best lot I'd ever caught with one draw. Of course there were thousands of rabbits on the hill before myxomatosis. The parkland was all gorse and we cut it into squares for the shoot, with two guns at each square. Twenty beaters beat the game. On 30 October they shot six hundred rabbits.

'I'd been rearing pheasants all the summer in a field near Benedict's Pool by the coppice. Arrow and Castle rented land off the Captain, my boss, for pea-growing. This year they planted peas near Great Hill, I doubt if peas had ever been grown before there. Nice friable land, mind, but a lot of stones. At the back of the field was the row of trees known as Grafton Firs and that fine ash tree known as New England. Below the Firs were the badger setts. It was alive with Old Brock and his family. Jack Fox used to catch the badgers in steel wire snares. He cured the hams like pig meat and sold the badger hair for shaving brushes.

'Arrow and Castle planted the hill with peas to come late in September when the glut of peas are over. Nearly one thousand feet up on the hill the peas don't get mildew like they do in the vale. The rooks from the rookery in the village played havoc with the peas in pod in September. Ponto was up there but never there early enough in the morning to scare the rooks away. Someone put poisoned bait down for them. Well, I was down by the rookery, which adjoined the village and the hall where the Captain lived. Seeing the rooks at breakneck, you know how they fly when it's going to rain, I didn't take much notice. Then all at once plop, plop plop, and rooks were falling from the sky into the road opposite the police station. I thought that the blame would be on me so I walked across the hill to the pea field and found out what was happening. Oh, the rooks left the peas alone after that but 'twas dangerous because I found partridges and pheasants poisoned among the rows of peas.

'The pickers came the following week, the diddycoys and the tramps, the folk from down town Cheltenham. The following winter when the hounds met at the Hall I did the earth-stopping early mornings on the hill and had a day with the hounds following on foot. Many's the time the mounted followers have given me a shilling for opening a gate.'

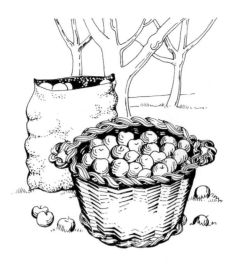

CHAPTER THIRTEEN

Bill Pitchcroft and His Sons

Cowmen and Cider-makers

In 1930, when farming in Britain was experiencing a slump, a 250-acre farm became vacant by the railway line and the brook. It was heavy clay land and no one locally wanted the tenancy.

Bill Pitchcroft and his sons had been farming in a small way in the Vale of Severn. He was a widower and what was known as a horse-coper. More than that, Bill was a cow doctor and amateur vet, using herbs from the hedgerow to treat sick cattle and horses. Bill decided to rent Carrant Farm at £400 a year, together with a large house and out-buildings and three cottages.

On Lady Day, 25 March, Bill, his two sons and one daughter, moved their horses and their wagons and machinery to the farm under the hill. The milking cows and young cattle came by train to the station in the next village. It was a sight to remember when Bill Pitchcroft moved like an eastern caravan to Carrant Farm, horses, wagons, drays, rakes.

By 1930 the more progressive farmers were using tractors for their ploughing and cultivating and half-legged horses for the hayfield and the market gardens. Bill Pitchcroft had no tractor.

It was five o'clock that spring afternoon when the little convoy arrived at the end of their twenty-five mile trek from the Vale of Gloucester. The sight of the sleek young shire horses pulling their load up the village street brought tears to the eyes of Tom Woodcock.

'It makes me think of times afore the First World War when our village prided itself with hoss flesh. That was the time when the mares were served by Bishampton Harold, fine foals he threw and so did the ones that Carburettor sired, the Winchcombe hoss.'

Bill Pitchcroft kept eight or nine cart-horses besides the colts he bred from the mare, His son Ern recalled: 'Our father was a widower, we lost Mother when we were at school and had a hard bringing-up. Tom's a couple of years older than me and Doris, my sister, younger. She has had to work in the dairy and look after the fowls. The farm down on the Gloucester Vale flooded every year with the Severn Bore and we kept Gloucester cattle for milking at one time, now we keep shorthorns.'

A couple of weeks after the Pitchcrofts arrived Ern asked me into the yard to see the cows. He and Doris had just finished milking the twenty-five shorthorns and over by the barn Tom was working with a steam engine. Inside the big barn a corn mill was grinding oats and beans turned by the flywheel of the engine. Bill Pitchcroft, with one of his horses pulling a cart, drew up alongside the cowshed. He was shovelling apple pomace into the mangers.

'Do they milk well on that?' I asked.

'Father makes a hell of a lot of cider and feeds the pommay, as we call it, to the cows. We brought this up from our last farm; nothing is ever bought for our milkers, that that we can't grow they goes without. We balance things up with linseed, that linseed meal do make thur coats shine. They be as slick as oonts.'

Ern told me with a smile of the 'outright', as he called him, a salesman trying to sell cattle cake to the old man. 'Our Father said we don't buy concentrates for any of our stock so you are wasting

Inside Tom Whiting's wheelwrights shop

your time coming here. "Oh, but the high protein rations we do," said the outright, "will increase the yield from your cows. You must keep up, you know, with modern techniques." Our Father told the chap to make off down the yard afore he let the bull out on him, and you couldn't see his ass for dust. Our cows do well you see, fed by the crops we grow, will milk for many years. Some shorthorns be twelve years old. If you force animals and their bags almost drag the ground giving big yields of milk, down they go with garget and you finish up with a barren cow.'

Ern Pitchcroft was proud of his horses too. 'Ah, they bean't collar-proud like some of us be on Monday mornings, they ull pull. I shan't tell you all what our Father do give um or else you ull know as much as we do, but one thing is their early morning bait. We grind oats and beans and cut chaff, this bait is moistened with pulped mangolds when they be full o' sugar after Christmas, not many, just a few. I come over to the stable about five o'clock with two slop pails from the piss pots from our house and next door. I pour this into the bait which has been made the night before and is warm, then the horses do have that for breakfast. The racks be allus full of clover. When I go to plough at seven the horses be nimble mind and they tires my legs by shutting off time at three o'clock.

'You have seen Father come past your farm with that cob in the trap. Well that cob was bought in Gloucester market for five pounds. He was a screw, a waster fit for the knacker man but Father fancied him, treated him with herbs and now he will come from Gloucester in under an hour. You see, Father used to deal with gipsies in the hoss trade and learnt how to treat ailments in hosses; it's a secret that will go with him to the grave. He won't tell me, no danger.

'Certain herbs Father do carry in his pocket attracts horses and he can catch the occudest hoss in the field. He'll walk around and keep talking to them and they be mesmerized like a rabbit is with a stoat.'

Ern then went on to tell me that there was talk of Mr Pitchcroft buying a Fordson Tractor and that his brother Tom was to drive it. The cider-making season was just started, Tom Pitchcroft was delivering the pure juice of the apple in 4½-gallon barrels with a Ford lorry. Ern then told me a little of the past history of Pitchcroft cider.

'Father has been making cider more than fifty years and he has got a good name in Gloucestershire. He never went to school for more than twelve months but as you realize he's long yudded. When the apple crop was short he used mangolds to supplement the fruit, then sweetened it with saccharine. That was in the First World War, but now he's particular and uses the best fruit and makes perry from Malvern Hill pears. The gentry buys cider from Father and prefers it to champagne.'

When the war broke out in 1939 Mr Pitchcroft reluctantly decided to buy a tractor. Prior to then the majority of his 250 acres were pasture which were grazed by his herd of shorthorn milking cows and young stock. All the heifer calves from the milkers were kept, and what a pretty lot they were. The white shorthorn bull on his red cows resulted in a herd of dark roan followers. One could call them strawberry roans. The War Agricultural Committee told the Pitchcrofts that they would have to plough up some of their pasture and plant wheat. The result was that the roan young heifers which were to act as replacements for the milking herd stayed on the farm but all future calves were sold for a while. Tom Pitchcroft first of all ploughed a pasture known as The Dean, twenty acres of stiff clay land.

'Our Tom, a good chap with horses and the steam engine for cider-making, was a bit mechanical for he delivered cider with the Ford lorry around Gloucestershire. Our Father gave him the job of driving the Fordson Tractor. He treated her just like a hoss. The paraffin from the tank was filtered through a sediment bulb to the carburettor. He was forever taking that apart and he called it the "sentiment bulb". He cleaned the tractor with rags and brushes, even swept the exhaust pipe chimney. I told him one morning "Anybody ud think thee wast a grooming hosses". Well the weather was kind and Tom was half-way through ploughing The

The tractor driver keeps a watchful eye on the furrow he is ploughing

Dry stonewalling in late autumn

Dean and he comes chug-chugging into the yard. It was tea time. Our Father meets him. "How's the ploughing, Son?"

"Oh, it's going pretty fair, Father."

"Well Tom, take her back after tea and carry on. The weather's kind and the dry wind will do the land as much good as a dressing of muck."

Tom replied, looking real worried, "Our Father, that tractor have done her shot for today. Her's bin working since seven o'clock this morning, her's done her whack and I don't want to maul her. I bean't a gwain back again arter tay. You be expecting too much, Father. Her unt hardly run in, it's not right to maul her."

'Father walked away, but I stood there laughing 'cos our Tom did think he had to treat a tractor like a hoss. Our hosses be got a bit long in the tooth now and Father's not going to break in any more colts. He's getting on a bit but he's got sweet on the housekeeper. There's no fool like an old fool and he's allus bin one for the women. Tom and me be working hard and Father's spending money on her, damn it!'

Having seen Mr Pitchcroft pass the farm every day with Maud, his housekeeper, it was noticeable that he had been smitten by the love bug. Dressed in a classy tweed suit, a pork pie hat with a jay feather in the hat band, and with Maud alongside in a fur coat, they made a picture as the high-stepping cob pulled the governess cart at high speed through the village.

Ern went on, 'My sister Doris used to look after the house besides working in the dairy, but when Maud and Father got together Doris had had enough and she went away. This woman off the Cotswolds was separated from her husband, a chap with a small farm near Stow-on-the-Wold. They had one child, a daughter of ten years old. Maud and her daughter came to the farm and lived in the house at Carrant Farm.

'I could see what was going on. Both our Tom and me were married by then and lived in the farm cottages. My missus had given me two young boys, eight and ten year old, and was expecting again. Every day Father went either to Cheltenham with his fancy 'ooman or Gloucester. Well, things didn't get any better; Tom was busy corn growing and I was with the cows. We had to give up the cider round because of petrol rationing.

'Then Maud's husband wanted evidence so that he could get a divorce. He was no fool and he was keen on citing Father. It was mid-summer, Father and his lie by had been to Gloucester, and a private detective came to the village with another chap. It was wartime and there were lots of fresh faces around. They were at The Wagon and Horses in the evening treating the village chaps and enquiring where they could borrow a ladder, telling the locals in the bar that they were going to pick the green walnuts off Doctor Richardson's tree. Albert Checketts lent um a ladder. Albert Hedgecock called 'time' at The Wagon and Horses at ten o'clock and from then on the detectives weren't seen again till the next morning. At about three o'clock in the morning the two men went up the ladder to Father's bedroom window and took a flashlight photograph of Father and his lady love in bed. Maud's husband got his divorce. It was in the paper about it. That was the end of Father at Carrant Farm. It ruined him – the divorce. Tom got the lorry on the road when the war was over and did the cider round and I took some land growing market garden crops and Father finished up living with Maud. Thur was no money left for Tom and me, but that's life!'

CHAPTER FOURTEEN

Jack Fox

STONEWALLER, RABBIT-CATCHER, ROUGH CARPENTER

Maybe I'm biased but I think there are no better walls in Britain than the Cotswolds' dry stonewalls. The stone is inferior oolite, a softish limestone. It does vary from quarry to quarry, the softer stone being easier to work with. Cotswold walls enclosed the fields long before the official enclosures. Bredon Hill being an offshoot of the Cotswold Range has similar stone. The main quarries were on Great Hill, Grafton Firs and Kemerton.

Jack Fox spent a lifetime stonewalling on Bredon, a dogged little man who thought nothing of walking the twenty-two miles to Cheltenham and back. Apart from stonewalling, Jack was a woodsman who felled the soft woods on the hill during the First World War for pit props. There was something special about this man, a confirmed bachelor, a gentleman when sober yet cantankerous when he'd been drinking. His tree-felling and woodworking tools were always razor sharp. One day he was carrying his seven-pound axe on the hill when his Irish terrier, Rough, ran under the axe blade and was slit along his back. Jack was devastated but he stitched up the wound and dressed it until it healed. He was so fond of that dog that when working on the hill he shared not only his bait with Rough but the tea from his can. Jack wore a trilby hat, which he used in order to give his dog a mid-morning drink. I suppose that Jack's trilby after years of wear in sun and rain did have a certain amount of waterproofing; the hat was partly filled with cold tea for Rough to drink from.

Jack used to call me 'Foreman' when I was a boy. 'Bring your hatchet over after tea, Foreman, and we will put it on the grindstone, I dare say it's pretty blunt.' So, as I turned the stone the little old man put an edge on my hatchet which was used to chop the kindling wood. 'Now I'll give it a whetting,' and Jack finished off the exercise with a whetstone.

Always genial with me, he would recite, 'Jack be nimble, Jack be quick, Jack jump over the candle stick'; then 'Johnny had a gun and the gun was loaded, Johnny pulled the trigger and the gun exploded.' I liked Jack's maxim, when he had told a tale he finished by saying, 'That's the truth and the truth needs no study.'

On the adjoining estate a gang of four men were engaged stonewalling. Sometimes they were repairing old walls, but the estate also required new walls to enclose the sheep walks. The foreman first thing in the morning threw his stone hammer as far as he could along the line where the wall was to be built. Where the hammer fell, that's as far as the men were told to build that day.

Here Jack, with his dog Rough, spent weeks at a time building walls. His dog had a wonderful nose for rabbits, he would sniff the entrance to a rabbit warren, then by instinct start and dig with his claws some feet away over the rabbits. Jack dug a few spits of soil where Rough indicated and got a good dinner for his efforts.

When Jack was stonewalling on the hill he never drank cider. With a heap of dry gorse to set alight to for a fire, he cooked the home-cured fat bacon on a nut stick to go with his dinner. It seemed that the sessions of cider-drinking were sparked off by some incident at his lodgings with his landlady. It was then he started at the Wagon and Horses with cider from his quart pot and came out with the saying to Albert Hedgecock, the landlord, 'Them two tots on the mantelpiece be just alike, specially that one.'

As men bragged about having good eyesight and Broadway Tower was six miles away, one chap said, 'I've just seen a fly on Broddy Monument.' Jack countered with, 'I've just seen him wink his eye.'

As regards snaring rabbits, Jack Fox has never been equalled. As a boy, I hammered in the pegs behind him as he set the wires. I set four near a little bridle gate on the hill one afternoon. After dark we went up there, every snare held a rabbit. Making the wires himself and camouflaging the new brass by smoking it over a wood fire was something only experience and studying the ways of nature could teach a man. Along a row of pines known as The Firs were the badger setts. The rabbits caught in the wires were easy prey for badgers and often they took their pickings before we arrived with the bag. Badgers are clean animals, so particular. They change their bedding quite often and when they take a rabbit they skin it before eating it and leave the skin.

Rightly or wrongly, Jack used to snare badgers sixty-odd years ago. He used steel wire, but no peg driven in the ground would hold this strong animal; the wire was fastened by a chain to an elderberry stool or stump. The badger's neck is thick and stiff, so Jack made a noose of the snare big enough for one front leg to go in the noose. He caught some quite large animals and dispatched them with his gun. Badgers are protected now and hopefully Brock is safe from the snares and above all the cruelty of badger-baiters.

Jack Fox was persuaded by his nephew, George (sprout-picking champion), to attend chapel at the neighbouring village. The chap who blew, or pumped, the chapel organ was a friend of Jack's. He had a cider mill and all the winter he made cider for the farms of the village. Jack only went to chapel on one occasion. His excuse for not attending was that he could smell the cider from the organ blower all through the service. It gave Jack a thirst and inevitably there followed a walk to The Wagon and Horses and the beginning of another session.

In later years Jack rented a barn in the village where he took on the craft of a rough carpenter. 'My old legs couldn't carry me to

Carpenters at work with a pit saw

the stone walls of Bredon Hill. The walking was more tiring than the stonewalling! So I set up shop in the Old Cross Barn. It was here that Dick Miles had had a wheelwright and blacksmith's shop fifty years ago. Dick made a bike and used to ride a penny farthing at the flower shows. Ah, he rode the bike to London afore the railway came. I took over some of his tools, but he was a proper tradesman. Still I picked up quite a bit of carpentry. You have to have an eye for timber. When I put a new shaft on a wagon for Harry Castle or Frank Moseley the timber had been seasoned in the barn for years. If I saw a good straight ash I'd cut it, that would make a shaft. Now for scythes that needed a stale or handle – we called it a sned – I always had my eyes open along the hedges, 'cause the branches of a tree bending the right way were just right. They are steamed and bent in the factory now, but I can spot one in the hedge already bent the right way.'

'Another thing, I started making tall ladders for fruit picking, light ladders about thirty rounds (rungs). Two larch poles, well one pole sawed into two, for the sides of the ladder, the rounds I made with ash or apple wood. They used to sell at one shilling and sixpence a round, a twenty or thirty round ladder would be two pounds five shillings.

'Did you ever hear of Tommy Dyke and his watercress ladder? He used to brag that the ladder had four rounds and that he stood on the middle one when he was watercressing.

'Of course, my nephew, Tom, used to make a big thing every autumn buying, packing and marketing blackberries for the women who picked from the hedges. The hedges were loaded with berries but our Alice, my niece, was but a little girl and couldn't reach the best berries on top of the high bushes. Well, most of the women and the wenches couldn't. I made her a blackberry ladder, what dos't think of that, Foreman? I made it light for her to carry. It was eight rounds and our Alice's blackberries were the best from the top of the bushes. There is always a way to get round things if you think it out.'

'What about recreation, apart from outdoor quoits at The Wagon and Horses, Jack?' I asked.

Jack replied, 'Albert Checketts used to keep the pub in those days. We played quoits in his orchard. Many's the time I've bin sent up to the brickyard with a muck cart to fetch clay for the quoit pitch. You see we stood back about fifteen yards and pitched the quoit rings, trying to hook the pin in the middle of the clay bed. When the ring landed on the clay that was a score. It's all finished now, but I believe the Americans still pitch hoss shoes.

'You know I told ya that I've no time for chapel on the Sunday like Tom and George do. I go out with me gun pigeon-shooting all the winter. When the hard weather makes um hungry that's the time to get the pigeons. They come in in thousands on the turnips and sprouts and cabbage. I make what we call a cave (a hide of branches and twigs in a deep ditch and get in there before it's light on a Sunday morning and wait. On a good day I can shoot maybe a dozen. They make good eating for me and my landlady and I sell some to pay for cartridges. My nephews, Tom and George, they be particular; I cut a cauliflower in the garden Sunday, they wouldn't yut it!

'You know, foreman, lots of folk go quite poetic about the skylark. They don't know what damage flocks of larks can do to a field of cabbage. They will strip a field like pigeons. Master Castle asked me to go and shoot larks in Hempits. I shot a lot one Sunday. We had lark pie, it was beautiful! I got a good landlady who's a clever cook. If only her didn't upset me at times about my cider drinking. She's strong chapel but, as I told ya, it's not good me going only to smell the cider!

'Don't forget, when the hatchet gets blunt bring it along to the barn, Foreman, I'll put an edge on him.'

CHAPTER FIFTEEN

William Justy

YEOMAN FARMER

The Cotswolds, apart from the main range of hills which stretch from near Stratford-upon-Avon to Bath, have lots of off-shoots. Under such a little hill lived the Justy family: two bachelors and their spinster sister. William Justy I knew as a breeder of Shire horses and a traveller of stallions. His one black stallion named Carburettor was well-known in the district; his offspring at three years old pulled the plough after the cart mares foaled some of the best colts and fillies in the two counties.

Apart from the heavy animals which cultivated the Midlands and south-western clay, Carburettor sired hunters, and their colts and fillies were the ride and drive horses of the heavy farmers. Apparently a stallion named Harold was an ancestor of Carburettor. I met William Justy for the first time on a May morning when he was walking with his stallion on his way to a hamlet under the hill. At ten years old I had just learned to ride a bicycle. Coming towards me was a short and stocky man dressed in breeches and leggings with a black and white check waistcoat, leading an enormous horse, Carburettor, on the right-hand side of the road. I

A farmworker inspects the thatch on one of the outbuildings

had been taught to ride my bike on the left-hand side of the road. there was a gap between the stallion and the grass verge and this is where I steered. William swiped at me with his stick and called me something not very complimentary.

'You're on the wrong side of the road,' I shouted.

When I told this story to Dad he told me that William Justy was quite right in the way he led his horse. If the horse was frightened by the traffic it would jump away from the leader.

Weeks later at the local market William was there with his stallion, showing it off to the farmers and exercising it up and down outside the market. Its coat shone, its great hooves clip-clopped over the rough limestone road; the brass on its mullion, or bridle, was like gold. Here was perfection in horseflesh, bred by William with careful selection.

Next year, William brought Carburettor to our farm and he served Flower, a liver chestnut mare; the colt Turpin was perhaps the biggest gelding on the farm when he grew up. I wasn't there when William came with 'the entire' as some called stallions. At eleven years old that part of the farming scene was not for me.

Stories about William were told by the farm folk of the day. William was a yeoman farmer, a gentleman it's true, but he worked with his two men from dawn until dusk. I suppose little stocky men and bachelors are a butt when the neighbouring farmers talk over their pint in the pub. William was not a pub person, but a devout Methodist who at the village chapel met the local preacher at the door, candle in hand, on winter Sunday evenings. He entertained the preacher to tea, stabled and fed and watered his trap horse.

It is said that William took Carburettor to one farm and as usual he had his terrier dog with him. The stallion served the mare; the dog served a bitch in the farm yard; and William got amorous with the servant girl. It resulted in the mare having a foal, the bitch had puppies, the servant girl had a baby boy; three jobs in one day!

A friend of mine, a local preacher, used to have tea with William. He said 'twas like going back in time' to visit this man who was then in his late eighties. The shorthorn herd had been pedigree since William was a youth. He spoke of his father threshing corn with horses before they used the steam engine. When the railway came in 1864 William fetched coal for eleven shillings and sixpence a ton from the local station.

My friend watched William on summer Sundays after chapel drive a flock of turkeys from his stubble field to the turkey house. William and his sister would top the market with their birds at Christmas, the bronze turkeys of yesterday.

One day, unfortunately, this kind of farming had to end – William, who had ridden to hounds, kept the pantry supplied with the partridges off the stubble, and who had made hogsheads of cider and perry in the old-fashioned way (a little pony turning the stone on the trough of cider apples, then the juice pressed and the pomace used to bank up the labourers' fires in winter) – his time would be over, but not for a few more years.

The tree-shadowed stone farmhouse in the woods had been a hive of industry, but the arable land now reverted to pasture. The house inside didn't change; the pot hook swung the big iron kettle over the fire to heat the water for tea. In the spring the scent of lilac came through the mullioned window as the logs burned on a bed of ashes and William told his story in his musical dialect, but winter evenings round the fire were when William was at his best.

William had a tradition of celebrating his birthday at mid-summer, and when the prospect came of his being one hundred years old and receiving a telegram from the king, he held a party in the garden. The farm had now ceased to function.

Under the elm trees the implements of old-time farming rusted among the nettles; the cattle stalls were empty and the turkeys had gone. Just photographs of Carburettor reminded William of his famous stallion and the hundredth birthday party was celebrated. Neighbours had mown the lawns, the flowers were all in their summer splendour; the trestle tables were loaded with the best farmhouse fare, his sister only two years his junior had baked a birthday cake. William in check suit and linen waistcoat spoke for a while, replying to a toast. He spoke of harvests, of yields of

Powerful horses pull the hay rake

grass, of wet summers, of marriage which he told the party he had never bought a ticket for. The party that year was on a Sunday. A friend said, 'I'm going to take your photo, William.'

William replied, 'not on a Sunday you don't.' The photograph shows William with his hand across his face; here was religious conviction, a man of principle.

'Shall I read to you?' my friend asked William Justy.

'Yes,' he replied.

'What shall I read?'

'Just read from that book over there as big as a stable door. Read I Corinthians, Chapter 13.'

My friend read:

Though I speak with the tongues of men and of angels, and have not charity, I am become as sounding brass, or a tinkling cymbal. . . .

When I was a child, I spake as a child, I understood as a child, I thought as a child: but when I became a man, I put away childish things.

For now we see through a glass, darkly; but then face to face; now I know in part; but then shall I know even as I am known.

And now abideth faith, hope and charity, these three; but the greatest of these is charity.

This could be called William's testimony on his hundredth birthday. It was his last party, the following winter he died. The house remains, the walnut tree, the old perry pear trees, but William is remembered.

CHAPTER SIXTEEN

Jacob Thorn

THE HERMIT OF PARSONS FOLLY

Jacob, a native of a vale market gardening town, lived as a young man in the back streets, where his wife had eleven children, childbirth had been an annual event; a typical late Victorian family. He left his wife and family early in the century to become the Hermit of Parsons Folly. With a struggle his wife brought up her family and five of the boys served with distinction in the Army in the First World War.

The summit of the hill where the tower known as Parsons Folly stands overlooking the vale is 960 feet high. The tower of 40 feet, built by Squire Parsons at the end of the eighteenth century, makes the view from it 1,000 feet above sea level. Jacob came here as custodian of the tower, living in the barn nearby, where the owners of the estate had built a fireplace. Here, next to the Iron Age camp with its earthworks, Jacob lived for nearly forty years.

Yes, he was an eccentric character. A giant of a man who put the fear into me in 1927 when, with my brother and another boy, I asked him to let us climb the stone staircase to the top of the tower. He chased us down the hill because we had not got the twopence he demanded.

*The King and Queen stones which were credited with magical powers stand near the
summit of Bredon Hill*

*Jacob Thorn became the custodian of the tower
known as Parsons Folly*

103

Jacob the Hermit could be a rather frightening figure, especially to local children

The Banbury Stone on the hill is an enormous outcrop of oolite; it was said to be a sacred altar used by the garrison of the camp. The King and Queen Stones, again near the summit, are pillar-like rocks, natural outcrops yet looking like human forms. A manorial court used to be proclaimed at the King and Queen. It was a custom to whitewash Their Majesties and pass sick children between the two pillars for healing purposes, especially for diseases like rickets.

Jacob the Hermit, living in a barn between the tower, the Banbury Stone and the King and Queen Stones, was steeped in the folklore of the hill. It seems that this and the Druids who cut the mistletoe with their sickles had an effect on the Hermit.

He lived on the produce of the land, and shared his living quarters with a Gloucester Old Spot pig. A pallet of grass served as a bed for the hermit. In winter he had a fire of gorse and wood to boil his kettle and iron stew pot. Rabbits, fine rabbits, fat off the wild thyme pastures, were plentiful on the hill. It has been said that the Hermit ate the rabbits raw; maybe, but I'd think that in the barn with the chimney stack he cooked them.

My recollections of him are dimmed by passing years, but that Sunday when we encountered him it was a frightening experience. Unshaven, wearing a smock frock, grubby cord trousers with the leather Yorks below his knees, he had a wild, faraway, look on his face. In winter he didn't wash but anointed his body with badger fat and pigs' lard to keep the cold out.

In the woods around were badgers. Jacob snared these with wire snares he made himself, a larger version of rabbit snares. He anchored the snares to the elder bushes. The badgers he killed and dressed like a pig and salted the sides of badger bacon. The hams were said to be quite delicious.

You may well say that one can't possibly live on meat alone. Blackberries in season and the large ketchup mushrooms were part of his diet. Every weekend he walked to the village at the foot of the hill, coming back with a sack full of bread and from the butchers he bought dripping. He had the strength of a giant and when Jarvie the pig-killer killed his pig he even drank the blood.

Here where the summers were idyllic and the winters bleak Jacob not only survived but he thrived. The question is often asked why Jacob was in such good odour (an unfortunate word) on the estate. The estate agent was always concerned about him. the owners of the estate, being bankers, created a rumour, quite untrue, that Jacob had lots of money in their bank. They were very good to this man who was equal to two men in the harvest field. When the oats were being carried on the hill Jacob was one of the best pitchers. Other men pitched the sheaves one at a time but the Hermit would stick his shuppick, or fork, into a whole stook of sheaves and pitch them onto the wagon.

As Jacob looked over the Midlands counties, the vale and river below, the Malverns not far away, I wonder what his thoughts were. He did visit his family some Saturdays, but wasn't welcome either in the house or the pub; he smelled of badger fat. His situation as a monarch of all he looked over was what he wanted. The folk around the hill accepted him. He walked to their houses with presents of rabbits and mushrooms, and at night raided the fishpond at the Hall for carp. It's said he ate these raw with blackberry jam!

The Christmas of 1927 saw a dreadful blizzard on the hill. There was great concern in the vale about the Hermit. On 29 December a party led by the estate agent visited Jacob's barn near the tower and found him well and in good spirits after a Christmas alone with huge drifts of snow filling the deep trenches of the Iron Age camp.

In 1934 Jacob's health deteriorated. The ulcers on his legs became crippling for him. After walking with the aid of sticks Jacob consented to go to hospital. He was soon back on the hill but died at La Lu, a little farmhouse away from the tower on 28 December, 1934.

It was the end of an era; the tower had been in the keeping of the Hermit for forty years. After his death the door at the foot of the stairs was locked.

CHAPTER SEVENTEEN

The Wireless

In the early 1920s Percy Perry, a retired engineer and brother-in-law of the Vicar, had been experimenting in making crystal wireless sets. This ex-Birmingham man drove a Douglas motor-bike and side-car around the hill villages. During the First World War Percy, being quite taken aback by petrol rationing, converted his motorbike to burn paraffin. Working on munitions in Birmingham and with his sister living Under the Hill, Percy reckoned to spend as much time as possible in the country.

Percy had mixed success with his experiments, and the village folk took his claims with a pinch of salt. Meanwhile a gramophone shop in town was selling three-valve wireless sets and Frank Moseley from Home Farm arranged for the proprietor, Sam White, to give a wireless concert. The village folk were invited to the hall to listen.

During the next few years everything would change: Big Ben would tell us the proper time, while up until the wireless came men adjusted their watches in the field as Beaches hooter blew for eight o'clock each morning. No one had imagined that the wireless would change the lifestyle of the country folk so much. It had not been in the thoughts of the cottagers that they would soon

Jim Arrow and his sister Lucy sit outside. The wireless aerial was attached to the end of Tom Arrow's barn

be hearing the news before work in the mornings and that their wives would be able to listen to music as they prepared the midday dinner.

The wireless concert signalled the change; folks would soon be listening in. Sam from town came in his Ford car that Wednesday in November bringing with him the magic of the wireless. Percy Perry met Sam at the recreation room. The gramophone man from town brought with him yards and yards of copper wire, the wireless set and insulators. First of all the set had to have its aerial and earth wires fixed. It was decided to take the aerial from Frank Moseley's walnut tree to Tom Arrow's barn. Walt Chandler, Tom Woodcock, George Fox and young Arthur Harris were in the yard at Lodge Farm.

'Where dost want the wires hitched too Master White?' Walt asked the gramophone man.

'The higher the better 'cos we are under the hill and we may experience oscillations,' Sam replied.

'Dost want me to climb the walnut tree for you?' Arthur volunteered.

'Well, if you could that would be good for the aerial,' was Sam's reply.

Walt smiled, he knew how Arthur could climb. 'Arthur's the best climber I've ever seen, for when we was at plough together many's the time he's bin at the top of the elm trees collecting crow's eggs at bait time.'

Arthur scaled the walnut tree and tied the aerial to the top branch. Young George Fox climbed up a ladder to the top of the barn and pulled the wire tight and fastened it, complete with insulators. The lead from the aerial went through a window into the village hall to the wireless-set on a trestle table. The earth wire came through a gap in the floorboards of the recreation room to the orchard outside. Here Jack Fox had dug a hole and Percy Perry had soldered the wire onto an old milk bucket. When the bucket was buried Percy watered the hole to get a good contact. Everything was ready for the great event at 5.30. Sam and Percy, after having tea with Edith and Harold, were ready to give the concert.

In the winter months concerts were held in that First World War army hut, known as the recreation room. Parties came from Evesham and Cheltenham; a lady from Dumbleton sang with feeling 'A Fat Little Fellow with his Mammy's eyes'; Frank Moseley, the farmer comedian, told his tales – simple country stuff enjoyed by all. This was different; it was to be a concert with no one visible performing – just a loudspeaker on a trestle table.

In the village hall after tea more than a hundred folk of the parish sat and watched the man from town with the wireless set. Three valves illuminated the set and as the two coils were moved to and fro groans and squeals came from the loudspeaker.

The programme began at 5.45, at six o'clock Big Ben struck the hour. John Henry and Blossom entertained, followed by Geraldo's Orchestra, the announcer being Peter Eckersley. The room was packed with villagers and when Percy Perry thanked Sam for his concert the applause was quite loud and long.

First of all Alf Blizzard, the shepherd, went to the back of the wireless set saying to Percy Perry, 'You aren't gwain to tell me that we heard Big Ben from London, 'cos I know that without the wind being south-west we can't hear Beckford clock strike or the bells from the church.'

''Tis radio waves, Alf. Different frequencies you see.'

Blenheim Hapgood said, 'Like as not it will upset the weather as it did when the clocks were altered to summer time.'

Jasper Hill, with arched eyebrows and yellowing ill-fitting false teeth, sucked his breath more heavily than usual, commenting, 'It udn't a done in the Squire's time. I won't be allowed to have a wireless, the missus ull see to that.'

'Why not?' Percy asked.

'I'll tell tha why. Hers religious and thinks that the gramophone is the works of the Devil. We have the *News of the World* but her don't let me read it until the Monday.'

As the villagers left, some asked Percy to make them crystal wireless sets and one or two ordered two-valve sets off Sam from Evesham.

110

A village football team for the years 1908–9

Eager faces await a trip to the 'Cup Final'

Jack Fox was busy weekends erecting aerials on larch poles from the wood. Harry Castle did one better: he got Arthur Harris to climb to the top of a wellingtonia tree to fix an aerial high up there. With a three-valve set the reception at the Manor was second to none. Previously Harry had used a crystal set supplied by Percy. He tells the story that one evening after a hard day in the hayfield he put the headphones on to listen to a news programme. He fell asleep, only to be wakened by the full force of a soprano singer. He wondered what had hit him.

Albert Hedgecock, landlord of The Wagon and Horses bought the biggest and best wireless he could from town and soon his pub was the hub of social life. Customers deserted other pubs to hear Albert's wireless and that's not all – women came to The Wagon and Horses! You see, their husbands were being entertained and they rightfully said 'Why not us?'

Percy Perry with his little petrol engine and dynamo built up quite a little trade in charging wireless batteries. the wireless had changed everything. Men who normally watched the village football match were now listening to commentaries of first division matches. The *Radio Times* marked out the football pitch in numbered squares. The ball could be followed as the commentator, Captain Wakeman, reported, 'The goalkeeper takes a goal kick, a high one. The ball's in square five. Now the centre forward passes it to the outside right, square seven.' It was all very interesting.

Tom Arrow put a long lead on his loudspeaker, taking it onto the lawn where on Sunday evenings the folk sat and listened to sacred music after chapel. One Saturday the villagers were thrilled as they listened to a broadcast of the Wembley Exhibition.

CHAPTER EIGHTEEN

George Green and the Allotments

There were two sites of allotments Under the Hill. The main one was a field known as Ayles Acre – or as some called it 'Hell's Acre', the land was so unkind, heavy clay suitable for brick-making. This enclosure was divided into seven or eight allotments of about four acres each.

The other site, on which there were five allotments, was a field known as Hill Withy; this lay alongside the railway line on one side and Carrants Brook on the other. It belonged to The Company, as everyone called the Midland Railway Company. Ayles Acre was church property.

During the twenties and thirties allotments were most unpopular with landowners and farmers. They reckoned that the allotment holders would tire themselves on their holdings and not give a full day's work on the farms.

Under the Hill the situation was slightly different, for some of the holdings were worked full-time by the tenants. They were known as Little Master Men and were often family affairs where the husband, wife and children all worked growing fruit and vegetables for market. One such family, the Greens, consisted of George Green, his wife Polly and daughter Bessie. George was a typical vale gardener brought up on the black soil of the vale. When he married, he was glad to take four acres of Ayles Acre as his holding. No way could he rent the fertile soil of the vale. Allotments, cheaper, were on difficult land as a rule.

In the garden of his thatched cottage George planted apple pips he fetched from the cider mill. The seedlings were normally cider varieties but George was an expert grafter. He used the seedlings as stocks for his grafts, growing some of the finest dessert and cooking varieties of apples.

If one has never seen a vale market gardener working on his land I'm sure something has been missed in the study of horticulture. On the clay he uses an Evesham two-tine digger, a fork with two prongs which have little spade-like tips. Many pictures have been painted of a plough team, two horses abreast turning a tidy furrow or four horses in line with a boy driving the teams. George Green with his fork turning the spits of clay soil and placing every spit in position produced a symmetry of upturned earth which can be described as poetry in motion.

George Green planted an acre of his holding with asparagus. In the early days of the allotment holders produce was taken to market by carrier's cart. To save paying the carrier, George wheeled his produce on a barrow to market. If the barrow was heavily loaded his wife Polly worked as a trace horse pulling the load over banks and hills.

George was very jealous of the strains of wallflowers he grew. He needed plants which would flower in the early spring to get the best price. A shrewd man, he noted the plants which were in bloom in February. Marking the wallflower with a cane, he left them to run to seed. By careful selection, George's variety was first in the market.

He also marketed Prolific Plums a few days earlier than his neighbours. Using an old trick he learnt from his father, he picked the fruit half-ripe, then covered the baskets of fruit with news-

Villagers proudly stand outside their row of cottages and beautifully cultivated allotments

A horse and cart move through the village at an easy pace

paper and stacked them around the fireplace. This system was known as stiving.

When he needed to sink a well for water, Jim Beckford offered to come with his divining tackle. 'No need for him,' George said, 'I know where the spring is.'

A patch of clover under the hedge kept green all the summer. It was here that George sunk his well, finding water at eight feet deep.

His land was always as clean as a new pin, no weeds. One year he had a disappointment, a late frost killed his plum blossom. A holding adjoining his was the land rented by Jim Harris. Jim, who worked on Frank Moseley's farm, had little time for allotments. The thistles grew high amongst his plum trees but his land was a bit higher than George's. He had a bumper crop of plums.

'Thurs no justice!' George said as he watched the Harrises picking the fruits.

The Parson commiserated with George, saying, 'How will you manage to live?'

'Read thee Bible, Parson, for didn't the ravens feed Elijah?'

After a bad day in the market when nothing was selling, Tom Fox who rented a holding next to George was talking to him. 'When ya gets down to the village, Tom, take a message to my missus, ull ya. Tell her that if I beunt back for dinner I'll be in the bottom of the well.'

Polly's answer was, 'Tell George to get in there if that's how he feels.' She told Tom that George was always making threats; he kept potassium cyanide in his cottage for tackling wasps' nests. If something offended him at home, he would reach up onto the shelf above his chair saying, 'Where's that tack. I'll finish myself off.' His family knew that he didn't mean it.

One Saturday Arsenal were playing in the cup final. They were his favourite team. Listening in on his wireless, he was upset when they were losing two goals to nil at half-time. 'They be useless. I shan't listen to any more of that,' he said.

He took his fork to the holding and dug all the afternoon. When he came home to tea it was to hear that Arsenal had won three goals to two. That was George, impetuous, but as a grower of the day the salt of the earth. Could his neighbours buy a little wallflower seed off him? Not likely, and I don't blame him. His selection paid him. When he had become established at Ayles Acre George bought a pony and cart for taking his produce to market, a comfortable five mile ride. Afterwards growers had motor bikes and box side-cars.

The little Master Men have now all gone. A tractor driver, unaware of George's well, went in with his front wheels and had to be winched out. I'm sure George would have laughed!

CHAPTER NINETEEN

Walt Chandler and the Wagoners

Early in this century wagons for farm use and road haulage were an important item in rural economy. Eli Thatcher made wagons and carts for farmers. He charged about forty pounds for a new wagon, which if looked after lasted a lifetime.

Albert Checketts, who rented The Deacle Charity Farm and lived at the farm known as Walnut Tree Farm, was a haulier. He used a couple of Eli's wagons to haul trussed hay from the meadows to Bredon Dock, from where the barges took it down the river to the Severn, then up to the Black Country.

For some time young Albert had set his sights on hauling from the branch line station at Beckford on to the Cotswolds. He took over this trade before the new railway line was built from Honeybourne to Cheltenham. Before then the north Cotswolds, particularly the town of Winchcombe and the surrounding villages, were dependent on Beckford station. The haulage was by heavy four-wheeled drays and shire horses. The steep hills past Winchcombe necessitated the use of trace horses.

Albert bought six drays employing six men. Walt Chandler, a young man about the same age as Albert, lived in a cottage up Cottons Lane. Five other men were enlisted in the team to drive the drays to the Cotswolds, but Walt was to be the carter or wagoner. Soon he acquired the name of Wag Chandler. His job was to look after Albert's horses and get them ready every morning for the men to start their journeys by seven o'clock. The horses, except in the winter months, were kept on Parkers Hill on the lower slopes of Bredon.

'I had to be up at half-past four every morning and get the horses in the stable by five, give them their breakfast and get them harnessed ready for the men', Walt told me. 'We gave um chaff, mangolds, ground oats and clover. They was fine hosses, as slick as moles in the summer, and mind they ud pull. The loads they took up them hills was sometimes a couple of tons.

'Albert had ten horses, some only three years old, but a couple of mares of twelve and fourteen. They bred some good colts mind. Master Justy's entire, Carburettor, used to serve um. It was a picture fust thing in the morning with me coming down the lane, the hosses had their halters on tied to the tail of the one in front.

'What sort of load did you take with the drays, Walt?' I asked.

'From Beckford some days it was groceries for the Winchcombe shops – flour, tea, sugar. It all come by rail to Beckford station. Then there was coal from the station yard. Beckford was busy then mind.

'You know what they says – "Back carriage pays", well we hauled all the jam from Toddington Factory to Beckford to go on the rail.

'That was jam from the fruit grown in Toddington Orchards. I know that Hugh Andrews, who succeeded Lord Sudeley at Toddington Manor, planted the highest acreage of fruit ever attempted in England. Hundreds of acres. You remember that Walt?' I asked.

'Yes, and the pickers who came from Shropshire to pick the strawberries and raspberries. They were all women who lived in the huts Master Andrews provided.'

119

G. Hayward's horse-drawn coach Perseverance *stops outside an inn*

A man proudly displays his 'tup'

Walt was silent for a moment, then said, 'A nice lot of girls always singing at their work. I courted one and some of our chaps got married to the Shropies.

'That was real jam from Toddington. The Bramble Jelly from the cultivated blackberries was my favourite. The foreman at the factory had been told to give some jam to the draymen. Beeches Jam it was, all fruit, no turnips in the jars.

'The five draymen I was in charge of used to come back about tay time if I was lucky. In the summer they was often as late as ten o'clock. I had to be at the stable to ungear their horses and give um some fittle, then turn them out. After days like that I didn't need rocking to sleep at night.

'Most in general I was sent on short journeys in the day so that I was ready for the chaps when they shut off. Albert Checketts used to send a boy to Winchcombe with a trace horse to be there to pull the loads up Sudeley Hill. That was when the drays were going to Guiting with coal. Then I went with the boy with one of the wagons to Assum Mill with a load of wheat. I remember we took about fifteen sacks at a time. That was an outing, 'cos Master Checketts allowed me to take the market gardeners straw to cover their radishes from the spring frosts. That was a help because they would pay me a tanner a bolting. Young Ned was the carter's boy, he used to look after the hosses while I had a pint at the Navvy, the Navigation Inn by the river at Evesham.

'When we went to Assum we allus put the horse brasses on the harness. Going up Bridge Street the little bell used to ring in the top of the mullin (bridle) and the brasses on the martingale was a treat on a nice day. On a frosty morning Bridge Street was slick and I'd have the filler's shoes roughed at the blacksmith's with frost nails in the shoes. We allus had a trace horse to help us up the bank.

'When Winchcombe station had a goods yard the business died down a bit, but we carried on in a small way drawing the Maconici rations from the factory in 1914. That was good grub, mind, meat, potatoes and vegetables all in one tin, but then I joined up in the Worcesters, was invalided out and went to work as carter for Tom Arrow and Harry Castle at the Manor.'

'Do you remember the viaduct collapsing near Toddington on Sunday morning on the new line?' I asked.

'Yes, course I do. We were there on the Sunday morning. It delayed the opening of the line, you know. That was the fault of the surveyor. Beckford station unt like it used to be before they opened the new line, but it's busy on market days with farmers and dealers loading cattle and sheep there. I've taken cattle there with young Ned for Arrow and Castle. The landlord at the inn wouldn't serve me with a pint of cider 'cos it was market day. He got more profit out of the beer. The market isn't like it was and most of the cattle and sheep travels by lorry today.

'I miss my hosses on those mornings coming from Parkers Hill down Cottons Lane; you would have liked to have seen us, six hosses in line all haltered nose to tail and me in front. They didn't take much catching by Shaw Green Gate. They knew that their mangers held fittle for their breakfast. We didn't always use the same six. If one got sore shoulders I had to doctor that with alum, and sometimes we would have a lame horse. There was no motor traffic. Then, one day, before the First World War, I remember a farmer from Toddington coming to Beckford with two bullocks drawing a wagon-load of wheat. That was a pretty sight.'

CHAPTER TWENTY

The Company

Some say the heyday of the railway was before the First World
War. It was a very vital part of transport after that war. The
majority of goods transported went by rail.

'The Company', as it was called, was spoken of with a kind of
awe in the 1920s. Anyone fortunate enough to work on the line, as
platelayers, as drivers, firemen or guards or in the booking offices,
were considered superior folk. One heard talk of the advantages
these folk had over the workers on the land. There were privilege
tickets enabling a railway man and his wife to travel cheaply;
passes several times in the year when they could travel free.

John Pumfrey came to the branch line station Under the Hill after
the Armistice of 1918. He was a dedicated Company man, I suppose
he would be called a gaffer's man today. He worked strictly
according to the book. The station was a busy one, both passenger
and goods, employing John as porter in charge and a young chap
under him who delivered telegrams. The station was controlled by
the stationmaster of Beckford who handled more traffic, and was
where Albert Checketts' wagons and drays did the haulage.

The villages Under the Hill were occupied not so much by
farming folk as by market gardeners. They loaded their produce at

the goods yard at the little station. John Pumfrey superintended the loading of the drays that arrived with the produce. A special rate for goods was charged for half-ton lots. Some of the small gardeners who were unable to put half a ton in the trucks shared the same truck with a neighbour.

'When I come to the station on what was known as "the Loop Line", John Pumfrey related, 'the growers were loading produce for markets up north. Some of them were unlearned men who could not fill in the consignment notes. I had to do that for them. One chap was forever asking for a new consignment book. I told him that I reckoned he was using them for lavatory paper. He was so annoyed that he threatened to report me to Derby. I gave him a form to fill in but he was quite unable to. Another chap loading bags of sprouts said there were thirty on his dray. I counted twenty-nine and put that on the consignment note. When he got back to his employer he said John Pumfrey had said there were only twenty-nine bags. What's that you are sitting on, the boss asked, and it was a bag of sprouts returned to the farm.

'There being no telephone in the village, we were kept busy with telegrams. My lad Ray was the link between the growers and the merchants up north. With his bike he not only took the wires, as we called them, to the villages but to the three neighbouring parishes.

'In the booking office when the men with the drays called for me to accompany them to the various trucks and vans they were intrigued with my machine which with dots and dashes spelt out messages on the telegrams. One often thinks of the telegrams in their buff envelopes as bringing bad news. That can be true, but the wires from Nottingham were for Arrow and Castle concerning the produce sent to market; for example it might have been "Good trade for sprouts. Send forty bags today" or "Plum market glutted. Don't rail any more this week."

'We loaded the 17-gallon churns of milk for Birmingham. Passengers waiting for the train watched as I bowled the empty churns across the crossing two at a time. We got used to this. Sometimes the Birmingham Dairy, Fullers by name, had a churn of milk arrive which had gone sour. This came back to our station

Two wagons resting from their use at the station at Notgrove in Gloucestershire

The station staff line up on the platform to have their photograph taken

on the Down Line and I made use of seventeen gallons of sour milk. You see I kept some pigs in the garden of the station house and Mr Arrow gave me permission to feed the sour milk to the pigs.

'We had a weighbridge in the station yard and the farmers made use of this to weigh the loads of trussed hay they loaded on the wagons. Bill Drinkwater had a coal yard alongside, he retailed coal with his horse and dray.

'The day excursions to Weston-super-Mare were popular. As many as a hundred folk would board the train for a day trip. Another popular half-day trip was to Cadbury's at Bourneville.

'I had one under-porter who was rude to passengers, I soon got rid of him. This chap was a teetotaller, dead against drink. George Moseley used to have gin come on the train in stone jars. I sent the porter up to George Moseley's house at Lammas Hey to tell him the gin had arrived. He said to Mr Moseley, "There is a load of the enemy at the station."

'When the line first opened in 1864, Jonathan the carpenter travelled from the next station. The stationmaster issued a ticket and when he arrived at our station he refused to give it in saying he had paid for it and was keeping it.

'Then there was the Rail Strike in 1926. You have heard that I didn't strike because my belief was that the strike would solve nothing. I kept the station open but no trains came and I spent my time in cleaning and painting the waiting room. I wasn't in the Union and never have been. Yes, there were nasty remarks said about me by the railway men but that was my principle and, as the saying is, my back's broad enough.

'The system has been on this branch line for goods traffic which has been loaded in the afternoon to arrive at market the next morning. A pick-up comes and with a little tank engine collects the trucks taking them to Evesham, where the ones for the north go into a marshalling yard and are put on a long train which goes to Birmingham; then they are split up forming trains for various markets up North. It's quite complicated but it works. If the produce is not in the market in the morning the growers fill a form in and claim compensation. Sometimes trains are delayed by fog.'

CHAPTER TWENTY-ONE

The Bright Lights

After a year of driving the four horse team at plough, Arrow and Castle gave Arthur Harris a two shillings a week rise in wages. Tom Woodcock, stockman on the farm, took on Arthur as under-stockman. His job entailed feeding the outlying cattle on the hill in winter.

'I can find thee a Saturday afternoon job along of Harold Perry working in the churchyard, that's if thee wants to earn theeself a shilling.'

'True, I do, 'cos Mother don't allow me a lot out of my eleven shillings,' Arthur replied.

'Now, my boy, don't thee becall thy Mother 'cos I 'appens to know what a struggle it is for her, poor 'ooman. Her got a big family and thee bist only one of two still at home.'

Arthur listened, then said, 'Oh hoy, hast got any more advice?'

'Yes,' Tom replied, 'Get theeself a bike and get into town instead of sitting in Albany Hill's kitchen smoking fags and listening to gramophone records.'

Arthur took Tom Woodcock's advice. All around in the mid-1920s a revolution was taking place. First of all the telephone came to the village and no longer did Arthur have to run to the station with telegrams for Tom Arrow. Prudence Hill was charwoman for Cath Arrow. She was petrified of the telephone. One day, soon after the telephone was installed, Tom Woodcock was at the back door of the farm delivering the milk to the Arrow household. He never forgot what happened.

'I heard a scream,' he told me, 'a really unkid yell as if someone had seen a ghost.'

It appears that Mrs Hill was doing the dusting in the dining room at Lodge Farm. The telephone was over by the window and as she was dusting around the receiver it began to ring. 'Mrs Arrow quick, quick, the tele bell's ringing,' she yelled. She ran into the yard where Mrs Arrow was talking to Tom Woodcock. 'Oh dear, Mrs Arrow, it's in the dining room. I'm not going to finish the dusting in there. It's awful, Mrs Arrow.'

She went into the back-kitchen and collapsed onto an old sofa there and burst into tears.

After the telephone came the wireless, and folk were listening in. George Cameron then made a village bus from a Model T Ford lorry. Every Saturday night the young up and coming youth of the day went to town to the cinema, The Scala.

Arthur saved a bit of money and bought a bicycle on what Tom Woodcock described as the 'never, never'. It was to cost two pounds nineteen shillings and sixpence. Arthur was liberated! It's true he did go to The Scala on Cameron's makeshift bus some Saturday nights, but on summer Sunday afternoons he fancied his chance on the river. He discovered that rowing boats and punts could be hired by the hour. Another of Arthur's part-time jobs was working in the house and garden for Doctor Richardson. The doctor's son Edward was described by Tom Woodcock as a gallus bloke. He kept a few cows and had a milk-round and furthermore he had a bike. On the Avon Arthur and Edward, two young what Tom described as 'hobbledehoys', took to punting on Sunday afternoons. While the young bloods from town were gliding along the river with their flapper companions, gliding and steering their narrow craft into the shade of the riverside withies and doing what Tom called 'sweet-hearting', Arthur and Edward were a picture in country corduroys. Arthur soon learned to use the punt pole, and he was also proving himself by roller-skating at the Drill Hall.

The year of 1924 was the year of a general election, a straight fight between the sitting Conservative candidate and Labour. In the early twenties anyone who voted Labour was considered to be either thick or to have Communist tendencies. Jasper Hill didn't care, he openly declared that he was Labour. He drove a coal dray and his employer was a Socialist.

Jasper rented out his front room on election day to the Labour candidate, Mr Robbin. Some of the working chaps who worked on the farms and lived in tied cottages thought it wise to vote Tory. They would come from the pub opposite and sing 'Who killed Cock Robin?' to aggravate Jasper who backed another Robbin.

The Labour Party did not, or could not, rent the school room for their meetings. The school board was Tory and Anglican! Mr Robbin spoke from the village Cross to a little knot of supporters. The result of the poll was a foregone conclusion and the only Socialist to win was Jasper, who earned two shillings and sixpence for the rent of his room.

In the village school that week the Tory member, Sir Thomas Davies, came and to liven the proceedings brought with him an amateur comedian, Cecil Bode. The school was packed, it was free entertainment. Two Labour supporters were there having refreshed themselves with beer at the Star – Jasper and Len, who worked on the railway.

'Any questions?' Sir Thomas said after his speech.

Jasper spoke up. 'When bist thee gwain to ask a question in Parliament? I've heard that the only time thee hast spoken in the last session was to ask for the winda to be closed because of the draught.'

When the laughter had died down, George Moseley the chairman said, 'That will do for tonight, Jasper.'

Len said, 'Lots of Parishes have council houses. What about our village, the last place God made on earth?'

A smart turn out was essential on election day

A gang of railway workmen at the entrance to a tunnel

130

Sir Thomas replied, 'I'll look into that with the local council.'

In 1925, a year after the dispute over the siting of the war memorial, Pedlar Price, Eli Thatcher and Sapper Norton put themselves up for election on the parish council. Pedlar plastered every roadside shed with printed election manifesto promises. What the candidate promised for the village! One of his slogans began 'Beware of the Wolf in Sheep's Clothing. They have deceived you over the District Council, don't let them deceive you over the Parish Council.'

It was obvious that the three left wing candidates stood very little chance of election. Who did they think they would replace on that five-man council? There was George Moseley, chairman, a landowner who had tenants in many cottages in the village; he was a good landlord, the rents were fair, and widows lived rent free. Tom Arrow and Harry Castle employed a number of the farmworkers; they were satisfied and would vote for them. Doctor Richardson was sure to be elected, the village depended on him in so many ways. Harold Perry was the only one who held a doubtful seat, but he was a generous man who helped the poor at Christmas and kept the churchyard tidy.

Eli Thatcher boasted that his family had served the village for generations; his father and grandfather had served at vestry meetings in the Squire's time. It failed to convince the village folk that the three men would be better for the parish than the existing council. In Tom Woodcock's words, Eli forgot to pay his bills, Pedlar was an atheist and Sapper was often fuddled by cider.

By the 1930s it seemed that the parish council had lost its grip on the affairs of the parish. More and more decisions were being made by the county council and the ministries in London.

'It will be a bad thing,' Tom Arrow said at one meeting, 'if the time comes when the land and the village is ruled from Whitehall.'

The land was going back to what nature intended. Ragwort, thistles and blackberry bushes encroached on the hill. Walt Chandler's horses were aged and were not replaced by Arrow and Castle. Only the best of the land was tilled, and that by Fred Woodcock on a Fordson Tractor. A new method of cultivation came to the village land.

The clay had been ploughed in the winter, the frost hopefully doing the work to get a tilth. If the land was ploughed in March and no more frost came to slake the clay land, Tom Woodcock used a Larkworthy scuffle or cultivator, an implement with nine legs, each leg with a sharp spear which stirred the plough land.

Clats, or clods, of clay described by Tom as 'as big as 'osses yuds' were left to weather by wind and rain. Four heavy horses pulled the scuffle. The land was rolled by a Cambridge roller, then scuffled again. After that, when the clats were reduced to the size of cricket balls, the land was cultivated by a heavy harrow called a Duckfeet Drag. This is how the heavy land was made ready for planting.

The new method now Fred Woodcock had his tractor made life easier. An implement called a disc harrow had been invented. The tractor pulled the discs over the ploughland and by continually crossing and recrossing the field produced a tilth. The discs were set at an angle and chopped up the ground. Old men frowned at the invention saying, 'it udn't a done in the Squire's time.'

Owing to the Depression arable land was no longer used to grow corn. Farmers became market gardeners, planting their land with sprouts, peas and beans. The vale gardeners had grown these crops for a number of years until their land became vegetable sick. They ventured to the land Under the Hill where the fields which once grew corn were like virgin land for sprout-growing.

Some farmers benefited by the new crops and, besides, the sprout stems and residue of the crops were good food for their sheep. The new system worked like this: the farmer ploughed the land and worked it until the tilth was suitable for planting the sprouts. The market gardener fertilized the field, then, in April, planted his sprouts. He vacated the land on 28 February after the crop had been harvested, paying the farmer so much an acre for the use of his land. No tenancy existed because the land was not occupied for a full twelve months. Land which had previously belonged to St Barbara's Church and had been administered by the vestry meeting now became the property of the county council. The council wisely divided the farm into county council holdings. This land was now used for market gardening.

Jim's brother Joseph Arrow with his wife in their best clothes outside their home. Note the aspidistra on the window sill

About the time Jim Arrow left the village Under the Hill there was an exodus of working men to the Black Country and south Wales. Wages were low, no more than ten shillings a week. Workers were wanted in the mines of South Wales and the ironworks of the Black Country. Joseph Arrow, Jim's brother, found work in Birmingham selling fish in the Bull Ring. It was a far cry from the village Under the Hill.

Revd Harrison and the vestry meeting recommended good working men for jobs away. Jack Chapel, Frank Moseley's wagoner, was a bit taken aback by some of his friends leaving the village. Some men emigrated to Canada. Jack asked Florence Moseley 'Where is this Canada? Is it anywhere in England?'

'No, Jack,' Florence replied, 'it's way out west.'

Jack thought for a minute, then said, 'Oi, I know what you myuns. It's Wales road.'

By the 1930s things had changed quite a bit. The Government gave subsidies to farmers so that they could buy lime and basic slag cheaply. There was a hint of war on the horizon. Men found work on the construction of airfields. The land with the aid of lime and slag began to improve.

Outdoor milking on the hill now meant a movable bail with a milking machine operated by a petrol engine milking four cows at a time. This invention of Mr Hosier, a Wiltshire farmer, was a breakthrough from conventional milking in a parlour. One of the advantages one saw on the hill was the fact that the manure went on the pasture; no cleaning out of buildings. A Hereford bull ran with the shorthorn cows. The whole outfit was operated by one man. His tractor moved the bail onto clean ground every day. Fold units each containing twenty-four hens were moved daily on the pastures. The difference these birds made to poor hill land had to be seen to be believed. The grass and clover thrived.

It appeared that the 1930s were the end of a way of life. Black and white Friesian cattle replaced the Ruby Red shorthorns and the crossbred shorthorn/Hereford beef animals became rare. Red and white cattle, which had for so long been the hallmark of Hereford and Worcester, were now no longer to be seen Under the Hill.

Glossary

adlund	headland at the edge of a field
anant	next to, opposite
Assum	Evesham
avions	a castrated stag
bags	udders
bobbety lanterns	will-o'-the-wisp
bothy	loft over a stable where labourers lived
Brumijum	Birmingham
burra	a sheltered spot, e.g. under a hedge or wall
the Chiel	a local column (no longer in existence) in the *Evesham Standard*
chaun, chauned	a crack in the ground in drought conditions
clats	clods of earth

diddycoys	gipsy-style travellers
Duckfeet Drag	heavy harrow with tines like duck feet
fit	feet
fittle	victuals
fother	hay or straw for animal feed
frail basket	a lunch basket, like a fish basket, made from sedge for farm workers
garget	mastitis
grains	the tines or prongs of a hay fork
hake	the front of a horse plough where the horses are hitched
hames	for attaching the traces to the horse's collar
hobbledehoy	neither a man nor a boy, a teenager
kerf	hay cut from the rick with a hay knife; a small truss
ketchup mushrooms	large field mushrooms for making ketchup
kibbler, kibbling	a mill to grind cattle cake into small pieces
mullin	bridle
old maids	horse flies
outright representative	traveller who calls and fills orders
oont	mole
oonty tumps	mole hills
plum bob	a piece of lead on a string to measure if a wall is upright

ranched	cattle which are allowed free range and are not enclosed by hedges
rot	rat
ship	sheep (Many upland pubs are called the ship, originally meaning the sheep)
shuppick	hayfork
skep	large wicker basket used for fruit or cattle feed
spits (of soil)	the amount of soil lifted by a fork or spade
staddle	the foundation of a rick
stales	the wooden handle of a hayfork
swath (swathe)	the grass cut at every circuit of a mowing machine
tallet	the loft over the stable for keeping hay for horses
teg	a yearling female sheep
tup	ram
unkid	unkind; unhealthy; not thriving animals or crops
utt	eat
waps	wasps
wick	week; a village near Pershore called Wick. Folk used to say it takes a man of Wick to walk over Pershore Bridge.
windrow, walley	several swaths of hay raked together

wires	snares
withy skip	basket made from withies or willow twigs
yaffle	woodpecker
yorks	straps put below the knee on workers' trousers
yows	ewes
yud	head

Picture Credits

All line drawings are by Sylvia Brace.

The majority of the photographs are drawn from the collections of Cotswold Museums Service held at the Cotswold Countryside Collection Northleach and are acknowledged as follows:

Gerald Drummond Collection, p. xv; Packer Collection, p. 6 bottom, p. 12 bottom, p. 17 bottom, p. 24 top, p. 41 top, p. 58, p. 62 bottom, p. 87 bottom; Glos Record office, p. 17 top, p. 79 top; Museum of English Rural Life, University of Reading, p. 24 bottom, p. 34, p. 93, p. 100, p. 125 top; English Folk Dance & Song Society, p. 72 top; Fox Photos, p. 87 bottom. Photographs on pp. 103, 108 and 133 are from the author's collection. The photograph on p. 104 is acknowledged to Alan Pye.